LIVING A LIFE OF YES

LIVING A LIFE OF YES

HOW ONE WORD CAN CHANGE EVERYTHING

DAVID RUPERT

ILLUMIFY MEDIA GLOBAL LITTLETON, COLORADO

Published by Illumify Media Global

Copyright © 2019 by David Rupert

> Paperback ISBN: 978-1-947360-24-2
> eBook ISBN: 978-1-947360-25-9

All rights reserved. Printed in the United States of America. No part of this publication may be reproduced, stored in a retrieval system or transmitted in any form or by any means, electronic, mechanical, photocopying, recording or otherwise, without the written permission of the publisher.

All scripture quotations, unless otherwise indicated, are taken from the Holy Bible, New International Version®, NIV®. Copyright ©1973, 1978, 1984, 2011 by Biblica, Inc.™ Used by permission of Zondervan. All rights reserved worldwide. www.zondervan.com The "NIV" and "New International Version" are trademarks registered in the United States Patent and Trademark Office by Biblica, Inc.™

Scripture quotations taken from the Amplified® Bible (AMP), Copyright © 2015 by The Lockman Foundation. Used by permission. www.Lockman.org.

Scripture quotations marked (CEV) are from the Contemporary English Version Copyright © 1991, 1992, 1995 by American Bible Society, Used by Permission.

Scripture quotations marked (ESV) are from The Holy Bible, English Standard Version® (ESV®), copyright © 2001 by Crossway, a publishing ministry of Good News Publishers. Used by permission. All rights reserved.

Scriptures and additional materials quoted are from the Good News Bible © 1994 published by the Bible Societies/HarperCollins Publishers Ltd UK, Good News Bible© American Bible Society 1966, 1971, 1976, 1992. Used with permission.

Scripture quotations from the King James Version, public domain.

Scripture quotations from The Message. Copyright © by Eugene H. Peterson 1993, 1994, 1995, 1996, 2000, 2001, 2002. Used by permission of Tyndale House Publishers, Inc.

Scripture taken from the New King James Version®. Copyright © 1982 by Thomas Nelson. Used by permission. All rights reserved.

Scripture quotations marked (NLT) are taken from the Holy Bible, New Living

Translation, copyright ©1996, 2004, 2007, 2013 by Tyndale House Foundation. Used by permission of Tyndale House Publishers, Inc., Carol Stream, Illinois 60188. All rights reserved.

Scripture quotations marked NLV are taken from the *New Life Version*, copyright © 1969 and 2003. Used by permission of Barbour Publishing, Inc., Uhrichsville, Ohio 44683. All rights reserved.

Scripture quotations marked (TLB) are taken from The Living Bible copyright © 1971. Used by permission of Tyndale House Publishers, Inc., Carol Stream, Illinois 60188. All rights reserved

"'Yes' is a dangerous word. Yet it is the very word that opens critical doors in life. David Rupert has written the book we all need to open our eyes to the power of 'yes' and spur us to action."
   Mark Foreman
   Co-author of Never Say No

"*Living a Life of Yes: How One Word Can Change Everything* is going to change the course of your life. Saying 'yes' opens the way for God to do what He wants in you and through you. David Rupert shows us that saying 'yes' is not about a religion, nor is it an activity. It is a relationship! David demonstrates how this affirmative response to God transforms lives. He gives examples of everyday people who've pushed through uncomfortable situations and moved past their fears to discover God in unexpected places."
   Stephanie Riggs
   Emmy Award–winning television news anchor
   Correspondent, Christian Broadcast Network

"David Rupert took a risk with his life and this book. Consistently obeying promptings for a year led him on the adventure of a lifetime. Reading this book to hear David's story – and the stories of others who said 'yes' – is more than vicarious entertainment. It'll prompt --- and equip – you to say 'yes' to the great things life presents you."
   Jeff Spadafora
   Coach at Halftime Institute, author of The Joy Model

"The simple word 'yes' is atomic: small but filled with nuclear power. Master storyteller David Rupert shows you how to access this power by *Living a Life of Yes*. The stories are true and the steps are simple. Without being preachy, this book will inspire and unleash you into a more abundant life. I dare you: say YES to this book . . . and then fasten your seat belt!"

Jim Walters
Executive Director, Servants of Christ International
Senior Pastor (retired) of Bear Valley Church

"David Rupert has some questions for you. Would you like to believe that your life matters? Do you have any personal dreams to make that happen? Are you willing to set aside your fears and take some chances to pursue those dreams? Do you sense God calling you to do something about these convictions? He also has your answer: YES!

"*Living a Life of Yes* documents numerous practical and profound ideas and examples of *Living a Life of Yes* learned from Rupert's life of 'no' leading up to an opportunity presented to him to visit the Middle East as a journalist during the beginning of the Syrian crisis and the rise of Isis in the region. His decision to finally say 'yes' changed everything and catapulted him into a completely different perspective of living, which this new book effectively and graciously details.

"So, get off the fence and walk through that slightly open doorway and follow David into the world of YES. It will change your life."

Jeff Johnson
Musician, founder of Ark Records

"David Rupert has perfectly captured the art of saying 'yes' to God. This book is a must for anyone who's tired of sitting on the sidelines and is ready to run with the purpose God has for their life."

Linda Evans Shepherd
Author, When You Don't Know What to Pray and When You Need to Move a Mountain

"Wondering 'what might have been' will only lead to a sad list of regrets, and that's definitely not the way I want to reflect on my life. In the end, I long to hear the words, 'Well done, good and faithful servant!'

"*Living a Life of Yes: How One Word Can Change Everything* inspired me to overcome my excuses, helped me to face fear, and encouraged me to step into the abundant life. And it all begins with saying 'Yes' to God's invitations."

Dawna Hetzler
Author, speaker, and founder of Jericho Girls Ministries

"For those of us who have gotten a little cozy with 'no,' David is there to wake us up with 'yes.' And he does it well. No annoying alarms here, just a warm (and very compelling) invitation to embrace the day."

Sam Van Eman
Author, Disruptive Discipleship

"*Living a Life of Yes* is a must-read for anybody who wants more from this life than they have—and that should be all of us. Saying 'yes' isn't about being proud or selfish—it's about stepping into the life God has created each one of us to be. Ignore the little warning voice that says maybe you should be careful, and boldly go where few have gone before."

Donna Schlachter
Author and storyteller

"*Living a Life of Yes* is David's powerful account of his own personal journey and commitment to say 'yes' to whatever God brought across his path. In David's journey to say 'yes,' he shares stories of others he encountered along the way who were also living a life of 'yes.' You will be nothing short of inspired and challenged to choose a lifestyle of surrender in faith to saying 'yes'!"

Anna Carroll
Founder and CEO, LightForce International Ministries

"David Rupert has broken the mold! While the world encourages a definitive 'no'—limit commitment, guard time and resources—this author, encourager, and motivator encourages a resounding "Yes!" In his life-changing book—filled with poignant stories and shared from a heart ten miles deep—Rupert encourages us to live and dream big, unleashing into our own life and others, the plan and love of God. Here's to a tremendous, bobblehead nod and a shout-out to *Living A Life of Yes*."

Jayme H. Mansfield
Artist, artist, speaker, educator, and award-winning author of RUSH *and* Chasing the Butterfly

"*Living a Life of Yes* by David Rupert will cause readers to call self into action and view their lives from a different perspective. For the majority of his life, Mr. Rupert lived a safe life, a life of 'no.' Once he began saying 'yes,' God was able to open up his understanding so he could see that life was more than living safely; life was about saying 'yes' so God could fulfill His deepest desires in the life of those who would be willing and brave enough to say 'yes.'

"My 'yes' took me into the US Army, to serve this country both on domestic land and on foreign soil. When I said 'yes,' I did not know where that one word would lead me. Neither do you, dear reader! If you want to move past mediocre and status quo, follow this YES-journey with David Rupert. Watch as your life changes into something that will cause you to sit up and take notice; something that will cause you to wonder why you took so long to say . . . YES!

Living a Life of Yes is perfect for Bible studies or book clubs. This is probably one of the best books to read in this new season of our lives!

"And the journey continues . . ."
  Beatrice Bruno
  "The Drill Sergeant of Life"
  Author, speaker, and US Army Veteran

"Does your faith life feel mundane or routine? It doesn't have to be. It can be exciting and spontaneous. David Rupert shows us how to live a surprising, fulfilling, and faith-filled life that goes beyond our imagination. If you desire a vibrant walk with God, start by saying 'yes' to reading this book. Discover how to embrace an attitude of, 'Here I am. Send me.' You will be motivated and ready to courageously say yes to God and step out in faith for the good of His people."
  Lori Wildenberg
  Speaker and author of Messy Journey

Every decision counts down to a single moment.
This might be yours.

CONTENTS

1. One Word That Changed My Life
2. Find a Way to Dream Again
3. Beyond Thoughts and Prayers
4. What's Your Excuse?
5. Moving Beyond Yesterday
6. Overcome the Fear
7. Don't Play It Safe
8. Get Ready to Change the World
9. Saying "Yes" Isn't Always Easy
10. Are You Ready to Say "Yes"?
11. These People Are *Living a Life of Yes*
12. The Book Ends, But Your Living Begins

ACKNOWLEDGMENTS

I'm forever grateful to my friends and family who encouraged this project. It's been a multi-year dream full of questions, probing and doubt. Your fingerprints of confidence in me is found on every one of these pages.

My writing coach Mike Loomis helped me formulate this message and gave me the focus to see it through. Michael Klassen of Illumify Media helped me with the technical details and carried the ball over the finish line with the right mix of pastoral care and professional guidance. Deb Hall of Write Insight isn't just an editor; she's a partner in the vision. Vanessa Mendozzi has great graphic ability, and she skillfully captured the emotions of this book.

My writing community, Writers on the Rock, is such a huge part of this journey. We started with just a handful of people around the table, and now we are a family of hundreds. You are part of the great cloud of witnesses who have cheered me on.

Carolyn Triano was my middle-school Sunday School teacher and helped spark my early spiritual journey. She also took me to my first writer's conference, helping launch my writing journey. Of course, I turned to her as an early reader, and I appreciate her insight. Jennifer Best has been an encourager to this vision, and she too helped with many of the theological and practical concepts.

When I needed friends the most, I counted on two men, Tim Orrino and Rob Geyer, who never wavered. Rob has been there since high school, and he gave critical guidance to this topic and my presentation. His keen mind and critical thinking kept this manuscript on track.

I want to acknowledge the care and influence of the pastors throughout my life -- John Scudder, Sam Worley, Scott Thomas, Vic Walters, Jim Walters, Chad Bruggeman, and Shawn Johnson. Each of them was a "yes" man, and they fanned the flame of trust and faith in me.

My family has been patient, loving, and supportive. My mother's influence in my life has lived on, continuing years after her passing. My sister Kathi always has a good word to say and continues to inspire me.

To my sons, James and Joshua, I pray that your lives will be full of wide-eyed adventure and that God will surprise you. To my step-children, Brad, Kate, and Malena. May your days be filled with wonder and blessing. To my grandchildren, I hope one day you read these words, and they will help you walk in bold faith.

To my wife, Lisa, *Living a Life of Yes* isn't a solo venture and you've been an amazingly supportive partner and friend. Let's keep taking the dirt roads.

David Rupert
Golden, Colorado

INTRODUCTION

"God has not given us a spirit of fear, but of power and of love and of a sound mind." 2 Timothy 1:7 (NKJV)

I've spent most of my life making excuses.

"No." "Sorry." "Maybe another time." "I'll think about it."

I took the easy road, avoiding people, turning down invitations, and passing on prospects. Life-changing opportunities were given to me, even thrown at me, and I politely passed.

After all, I had a family to raise. I had bills to pay. I had a career. All these things are fine endeavors, but I used them as convenient justifications to keep me from expanding my world.

I picked comfort over disquiet.

I opted for safety instead of curiosity.

There is no shortage of things that keep us busy. The everyday business of raising a family, making a living, and filling our free time with play and fellowship and friends fills the calendar. So, reading a book that encourages you to add something to your already full plate might seem counterintuitive.

INTRODUCTION

There is an inherent message in our society that encourages people to say "no" to protect their time, their wallets, and their hearts. There are plenty of agreeing voices, a chorus of others who encourage us to continue down this path. Parenting experts, spiritual guides, and time managers all embrace the word "no."

Tony Blair, the prime minister of England from 1997 to 2007, said, "The art of leadership is saying no, not yes. It's very easy to say yes."

I would respectfully disagree with Mr. Blair. From personal experience, it's far easier to say "no." "No" slips easily off our tongue like an ice cube on a summer day. We are conditioned to say "no" because saying "yes" means a commitment of our resources, energy, and passions. Instead, we just say "no" and move on.

Steve Jobs, the brains behind Apple, also was an advocate of "no." When speaking about a company's focus, he said, "[Focus] means saying no to the hundred other good ideas that there are. You must pick carefully. I'm as proud of the things we haven't done as the things I have done. Innovation is saying 'no' to [a thousand] things."

I get it. From a business perspective, a leader often needs a laser focus on the prize, no distraction. Ventures and deals and prospects come in like a torrent, and leadership sifts through them relentlessly. Most opportunities will be busts. Some could lead to a company's ruin. But think of all the great times Jobs said "yes," creating one of the world's most successful companies to date.

Even billionaire Warren Buffett says that "the difference between successful people and very successful people is that very successful people say 'no' to almost everything."

INTRODUCTION

These three men throw up plenty of reasons to dissuade you from accepting the message of this book. But let me give this appeal. These standards do not define our lives. I don't need to be Buffett-rich, Jobs-smart, or Blair-powerful. I'm here to say there is another path. The noise of life crowds out the still, small voice calling us to something more profound.

There are times when saying "no" is prudent and smart. This book is not a carte blanche to say "yes" to those things that will bring financial, spiritual, or emotional ruin. The "no" based on wisdom is far different than the "no" based on fear.

In these pages, I want to move you past those fears. I want to convey a different kind of living —one of everyday wonder, amazement, and surprise.

Sheryl Sandberg, COO of Facebook, said this: "If you're offered a seat on a rocket ship, don't ask what seat! Just get on."

A baby begins learning language with two words in his vocabulary: "Mama" and "no." From the very beginning of our conscious life, we are conditioned to start saying "no."

I am learning that I will never live an exhilarating life if the first word out of my mouth is "no." The defensive mechanism of pushing back and guarding my time, preventing myself from exposure to discomfort, is precisely the thing that keeps me from a life of blessing.

In these pages, you'll read the stories of ordinary people—many of them just like you. But they've decided to shed the shackles of a life of "no" and instead are embracing "yes."

I started down this path several years ago, and I've never lived a happier, more inspired life. The excuses are beginning to melt, and I'm finally *Living a Life of Yes*.

The "3-2-1" moments we all have faced in our lives, those

INTRODUCTION

times when we decide to jump in with all our might and gusto, are either our biggest regrets or our biggest successes. I'm hoping that as you read this book and you hear the countdown, the next word out of your mouth will be "jump."

1

ONE WORD THAT CHANGED MY LIFE

"That's what I mean: Risk your life and get more than you ever dreamed of. Play it safe and end up holding the bag."
—Luke 19:26 (MSG)

January 1.

It comes every year. The calendar page flips, and suddenly we find another new year is thrust upon us.

The month is named after Janus, the Greek god of beginnings and transitions. She has one face looking to the future and another at the past.

We ceremoniously mark the new year with a chance to start over. It's the traditional time of resolutions, of self-reflection. This one day of honesty is when we collectively and individually identify our weaknesses and resolve to fix them.

New Year's Day is the perfect opportunity to makes vows to spend more time with the kids, take a college class, or lose weight. We resolve to quit smoking, stop angry driving, and start praying more.

A modern twist on the traditional New Year's Day resolution is to adopt a single word or phrase for the year. I've been doing this for several years, identifying a label for the year, a concept that would define my life and give me focus.

Some people pick words like "forgiveness," "service," or "freedom." Others pick words like "consistent," "self-discipline," or "love."

The first word I ever chose wasn't particularly profound. It wasn't all that deep. It wasn't spiritual.

It was a simple word.

"Yes."

On that first day of 2015, I resolved to say "yes" to every opportunity God put in front of me. I would quit saying "no," leaning on the crutch of safety. Instead, I would leap into the unknown and give God a chance to work His wonders.

This vow to say "yes" would change my life.

Opening a New World

Since I made this commitment, it hasn't always been easy, but the rewards have been amazing. *Living a Life of Yes* isn't just a decision or a single pithy word. It's a lifestyle.

But to get there required one step at a time, every single one of them by faith. I often feel like a man walking into the desert without a plan, hoping to stumble onto an oasis of water, a road, or another pilgrim.

Along the way, I found God in the mystery. I found God in the uncertainty. I found God in surrender—surrender to "yes."

LIVING A LIFE OF YES

As I opened my eyes to what was around me, the world began to open up to me.

Ever since I made that decision on January 1, 2015, I've been living a life of absolute surprise. I've met people and gone places I would have never imagined going.

I've spent time in the Middle East, sharing tea with Christian families whose lives have been upended by ISIS. I've met with Muslims in the Middle East and America, looking for commonality and understanding of what drives hate.

I've marched with persecuted Ethiopians.

I've sat with African Americans who feel a sense of oppression.

I've spent time with a woman whose husband was martyred for his faith.

I've had in-depth discussions with atheists and Wiccans and fundamentalists.

I've broken bread with Democrats, Republicans, Socialists, and Libertarians.

I've started conversations with meth addicts, homeless women, and other individuals in forgotten circles of our society.

I've attended formal discussions sponsored by terrorism experts, NASA scientists, and gold panners, just for fun.

I've turned into a curious man, one who asks questions merely to gain access to new territories of people, knowledge, and experience.

I now embrace my innocence, no longer running from surprises.

Many of my friends who've known me for years are doing double takes. I was Mr. Conservative. I advised my friends to "look before leaping" and to be wary of rash decisions. I always considered the costs and labored over my options. I figured I could drown difficult choices by holding them under the water of indecision.

My approach to life was to sit down with a long legal pad and draw a line down the middle. At the top would be the big decision of the moment, and I'd list the benefits on the left and the costs on the right. I reasoned I could make each tough decision by determining which list was longer, the benefits or the costs.

But I've changed. I'm learning to experience God's riches, His profound blessing for this life, and I'm learning that I must leap—and trust. Faith isn't just leaning back and waiting for life to happen on its own. Faith is stepping out, walking and experiencing the unknown. It's that child-like trust that He will lead you into the right situation.

I believe by reading my story and the others in these pages, you'll start to live your own life of "yes."

The Accidental Pilgrim

It only took a few days to test my resolve. In fact, on January 5, 2015, my first big test of *Living a Life of Yes* came in the form of an email from the "Tourism Board of His Highness, from the Hashemite Kingdom." It was that regal. As I read on, I realized the offer was from the country of Jordan, asking me to research and write about the Christian heritage of their country.

At first I was intrigued, but then I looked at the map. Gulp. Jordan is in the Middle East, literally right in the middle of the Middle East. All the neighborhoods I've lived in have been defined by the neighbors. I've had some good ones. I've had some bad ones. Jordan has both. The country is bordered by Israel and Palestine to the west, Syria to the north, Iraq to the east, and Yemen and Saudi Arabia to the south.

It was kind of like buying a pretty house in a rough neighborhood. "It's safe, right?"

Throughout the Syrian Civil War and the uprising of ISIS throughout the region, dozens of journalists from established news outlets as well as citizen journalists have been kidnapped, imprisoned, and some even killed. No one would blame me for saying "no" based on this.

But the roadblocks in my mind weren't just about my safety. My self-doubt perhaps screamed even more loudly.

The qualification game I was playing was dangerous to my confidence. Who was I kidding? I wasn't a travel writer. I wasn't a Middle East expert. I wasn't an author with a substantial following. I was just . . . me.

I would join nine other writers with significant pedigrees and influence. Many were well-known national figures. I had no business being in this crowd.

Here's who I am. I'm a middle-aged government office worker who had little exposure to the Middle East beyond pita bread and Indiana Jones movies. I have a full-time job, family and community responsibilities, and writing has always been a side gig for me. I've run in writing circles for a long time and could name dozens of others who were more qualified.

Like Moses, I was hoping that God would find an Aaron to communicate His word. But I wasn't about to get off the hook that easy. One confirmation after another occurred in rapid fire, and before long I was committed.

I wrote these words before I went:

Why would the country of Jordan have faith that I would represent their country well, so much faith that they would spend so much to bring me there? There's no other explanation, except that God has a story and for whatever reason, I am supposed to tell it. I can argue with Him, telling Him that He's crazy. I can deflect and deny and deflate this opportunity. Or I can accept it for what it is. More than any other opportunity, this one rings of something greater. It's a pilgrimage to a story that I don't know. Like the wise men who simply followed a star and asked a few questions, what will I find?

I took a deep breath, remembering my vow. "Yes, God. I'll go."

An Introduction to the World

My reward was a trip to visit several Middle East holy sites. I stood on Mount Nebo, the very place where Moses looked across the Jordan River and God showed him the boundaries of the promised land. I went to Petra, the Lost City of Stone. Founded by the Nabataeans, it remains shrouded in secrecy since the civilization simply disappeared in the fourth century. Along the way, I visited Christian churches, some with congregations that count their history by hundreds of years. I floated in the Dead Sea. I spent an entire day at the baptism site of Jesus, relishing the rich church culture that venerates the site. I stood on the hill traditionally assigned to Elijah's encounter with the chariots of fire.

And I met Christians at every stop along the way, dispelling many notions about the health of the Christian faith in the Middle East. I felt like I was in the middle of a bigger story, one that was being written on the very soil I walked. I didn't know the title. I didn't know the beginning. I didn't know the end. Like picking a random library book off a shelf and reading the first page it falls open to, I was trying to find my place, my purpose.

I also met some other Christian workers in the country who introduced me to refugees. This was months before the refugee story took hold. I was fascinated. I learned about the ISIS push in Iraq and especially the targeted attacks on Christians and other religious minorities. I met some people who had been impacted by these terrorist groups; I heard their horror, admired their faith.

I also learned about the escalating Syrian Civil War. I met refugee children and couples who were hoping to navigate an uncertain future, trying to make sense of a world that seemed to be imploding.

Some of these people were battered, oppressed, abused, and persecuted for their faith. They were beyond the reach of the news, so they were unknown to me and many others in the Western world. Where I could retreat to my North American comforts, the dangerous edge was where they lived—hoping and praying for relief.

Little did I know that all this background material would later help propel me right into the thick of a worldwide discussion.

From Destination to Destiny

I came home and wondered what the big picture was. Was I supposed to be merely a travel writer, telling others how to plan their vacations? Or was there another destiny here, a deeper purpose?

I thought about Abraham, the first real Pilgrim, who "By faith . . . when called to go to a place he would later receive as his inheritance, obeyed and went, even though he did not know where he was going" (Hebrews 11:8.)

At the age of seventy-five, he found himself the patriarch of his family when he got a new instruction from God.

> "*The LORD said to Abram, 'Leave your country, your relatives, and your father's home, and go to a land that I am going to show you'" (Genesis 12:1 GNT).*

"[He] went . . . even though he did not know where he was going" became a phrase I could lean into. My life before this point had been driven by destination. Not so with Abraham. He didn't have a clue about the destination; he just said "yes" and pressed on into the desert toward his destiny.

And so, I resolved to join Abraham, to take on his level of trust, and to see where "yes" would take me.

I came home and started living a daily life of trust and faith, a life of "yes."

That first year was astonishing. Every time I said "yes," it would lead to another open door. And that would lead to another open door. And then when I said "yes" to that, another one would open.

All of this "saying yes" was preparing me for something I didn't—or couldn't—understand. It wasn't long before I found myself immersed in the epicenter of politics, humanity, and God.

Responding to the Need

Later that same year, refugees began to flood through Europe. Many of us were horrified at the images of people loaded into boats crossing choppy seas, of masses of people clogging borders; we were appalled by the photo of a boy in tennis shoes lying lifeless in the sand, washed up on a Greek beach.

People voiced their disbelief, blaming politicians, leaders, and just about anyone in authority, regardless if they had a horse in the race. The refugees were spawning conversations about immigration policy and the role of the United Nations and cross-cultural relations. In the middle of a US Presidential race, they provided fodder for debates and posturing. They became talking points regarding terror, fear, and compassion. They were pawns in worldwide political gamesmanship.

Many of my friends were wringing their hands, hopeless and unable to move. Good-hearted people had no idea how to reach people across the ocean with little commonality except the human quotient.

I was right there, feeling a little helpless myself.

And then I realized, this was the moment God had been preparing me for. Just a few months earlier I had been in Jordan wondering, "Why?" Now I knew. Stories about these refugees needed to be told. And now I had the background and the preparation to tell them.

So I put together a second trip to the Middle East. This one wouldn't be to the tourist sites. This one wouldn't hinge on my photography or my cultural analysis. This one would be to help tell the story of the refugee, specifically the Christian refugee.

I embraced the *Living a Life of Yes* mantra, resisting every urge to plan every meticulous detail of the trip. And right up to my departure, I didn't have a solid day-by-day plan. I didn't have a specific agenda. I didn't even have a budget. Just like Abraham.

By faith, I walked.

Living a Life of Yes means embracing the discomfort of the unknown, which is not always easy if you like to plan out your life.

Don't Spoil the Story

When I write a story, I must confess that I often have it "prewritten" in my brain. I have a title, an impressive lead, a few points, and maybe a conclusion. I work out the plotlines and the twists that lead to the explosive ending. And then I start to write.

When I started this next leg of my journey of "yes," I desperately wanted to develop a lead and an outline before I even boarded an airplane. I wanted to fill in the blanks along the way.

But God isn't always so tidy when He tells a story. His story is often told one paragraph, one sentence, or one word at a time. That's what my life has been like since that New Year's resolution.

I wanted to be true to God's continued calling, trusting him to open doors and lead me to exactly the right people.

For the first time in my life, the story I would live and write would not be formulated in my mind first. I would trust God, every single moment. I would blindly say "yes" to Him.

This journey would be different. I worked hard to be faithful to this.

The Missing Pieces

As I gathered up travel documents, clothes, and funds, I found I lacked a couple essential items: courage and conviction.

I knew I was supposed to be strong, to march up to the Philistine and plunk him with a rock in the forehead like my namesake, the shepherd David.

But to be honest, I was full of self-doubt. The big idea to head over to the Middle East and tell the refugee story was a bureaucratic mess. The connections on the ground were nonresponsive. I couldn't find a translator. The details began to dog me.

Instead of the warrior standing over the giant, I felt like the trembling David sitting in the cave, writing a weepy Psalm.

I woke up the morning before the trip full of doubts. What was I thinking? *Who do you think you are?* I asked myself.

I had a good idea where those thoughts came from. Still, they swirled around my head like they were right at home.

Then, out of the blue, a Facebook friend sent me a note. She had opened a book that she hadn't read in more than a year and found several large-denomination bills in the chapter titled "Overcoming Fear."

"The second I saw these, I knew they were yours," she said. "What a sense of humor He has."

Another friend sent me an email. "Keep focused on the promise." A third friend sent this message: "God's hand is on you, David. I know it is a bigger plan than you see right now. Go. Go tell the story."

Who am I to brush off the encouragement of people I love? Who am I to doubt the trust of those who give me money? Who am I to have misgivings about the timing? Who am I to question God?

Immediate Confirmation

I arrived at my simple hotel in Amman, Jordan, at 3:00 a.m. I had no idea what the "real time" was, but this was my new residence, my new reality—at least for the next couple weeks.

I couldn't sleep, and I was in the lobby at 7:00 a.m.—looking for food. And here's where I met Jack—a precocious twelve-year-old boy dressed in a soccer shirt and jeans. He made eye contact, and we started immediately conversing.

He wanted to know if I spoke English. Smiling, he was eager to test his schooling. With hardly an accent, he asked what I was doing in Jordan. I told him that I was in the country looking for Christian refugees.

He told me that his family were followers of Jesus and they were refugees from Syria. "You want to talk to us?"

Of course, I said, "Yes."

He brought his father, Albert, down to the lobby, and we spoke for a couple hours. I learned the family was from Aleppo, the once-beautiful Syrian city laid siege by government forces and rebels.

Albert told me stories that were hard to hear. In Aleppo the rebels had cordoned off the Christian portion of the town, and snipers were picking off civilians. To get the children to school, Albert and his wife would split the children up. That way, there would be a parent who would still be alive to parent the surviving children in the event of a shooting.

They persevered in Aleppo for a couple years, hoping the war would end. With multiple forces fighting for control of the city,

Albert couldn't take sides, except if necessary, to protect his family. After a bomb exploded in front of their house, Albert had had enough. That was the last close call. He gave up his business, his career, and took his family across the Jordanian border.

I wrote about Albert and his family, and published the story at Patheos.com, the world's most widely read religious website. The story went around the world, read thousands of times in dozens of countries. It was quoted in several publications and was a unique and early insight into the victims of the Syrian conflict. Few had considered the hundreds of thousands of Christians who were impacted, lost in the confusion of shifting alliances and confusing politics.

Later, Albert printed out the story I had written about his family, and it accompanied his immigration paperwork; he showed it to officials and aid workers to help explain their plight.

They are now in Canada. These Arabic-speaking Assyrian Protestants were adopted by a Chinese-speaking French-Canadian Catholic parish. Life for them is now so much different.

And so it went. Every day I was in Jordan, I would wake up in ignorance and trust that God would lead me to the stories He needed me to tell. They came in rapid succession.

I met and wrote about an Iraqi soldier who helped hunt down Saddam Hussein and later found himself targeted by ISIS. Now he was a refugee.

I wrote about a young couple from Mosul, Iraq, who were targeted by ISIS for their faith, the sign of the Nazarene painted on their porch.

I met a man whose father was killed by rebels fighting the Syrian Arab Army. He was ready to go back and fight, but because of an encounter with God, he renounced his vow for vengeance. I later watched him get baptized in the Jordan River.

I wrote about a young couple whose wedding was interrupted by the ISIS invasion of their hometown in northern Iraq. They stole away into the night, two young lovers on the run. They later found a priest in southern Turkey who married them in the courtyard of his church.

There were dozens more stories to tell to a world that was hungry for answers, for clarity, for direction.

Even though I started the trip in complete ignorance, I was able to report knowledge from a first-person perspective. This *Living a Life of Yes* was beginning to take shape and reveal a purpose.

In the German language, the word *Sehnsucht* doesn't have a direct English translation. But C. S. Lewis framed it as "the inconsolable longing in the heart for we know not what." And when that longing is fulfilled, the soul awakens and the surge in emotions is what Lewis calls "joy."

That's what I was feeling: a sense of meaning. Little did I know that finding the joy of my calling would be in the middle of such human tragedy.

I Had a Voice

Within a week of my return, the terrorist attacks in Paris happened. Three suicide bombers struck a soccer stadium, followed by several mass shootings at cafes, restaurants, and concert venues. One of the attackers was a refugee from Syria. The terror struck fear in the hearts of people everywhere.

The entire world was wringing their hands, uncertain of what to do. Governments and politicians and the internet were on fire. And here I was, right in the middle of it. I was able to help tell the stories with clarity and conviction. I had something to say—because I had looked at people from this region in their eyes and heard their firsthand accounts.

Throughout the crisis, I contributed to the national discussion through writings, interviews, talk shows, and presentations. I was someone who spoke with authority.

For all the decades prior, I hadn't made my mark on this planet. Finally, my words meant something. My actions could impact lives. By stepping out in faith, I saw my life move from the suburbs to the middle of a firestorm.

I know some of this is dramatic, and I know you may be thinking about "checking out" of this idea. War zones, the Middle East, and foreign cultures are too much of a stretch. I get it and don't blame you. But I needed to tell you about this first year of *Living a Life of Yes* so you'd understand why I'm so passionate about the subject.

That's my extreme. Yours might lead you to start engaging with a different culture in your community, a new circle of friends at work, or a neighbor who doesn't look like you. Opening yourself to "yes" possibilities won't necessarily send you across the world, but it might send you across the street.

I've been saying "yes" in everyday decisions, and along the way I've gone to many new places, met countless interesting people, and explored wildly different perspectives.

Suddenly, I am alive.

The Sehnsucht that you feel in your own life is the same calling we all have. It's the draw to a deeper purpose, the ability to make a difference and live a life of impact.

How can you start to live this life? It begins with learning to dream again.

2

FIND A WAY TO DREAM AGAIN

"So many of our dreams at first seem impossible, then they seem improbable, and then, when we summon the will, they soon become inevitable."
—Christopher Reeve

Living a Life of Yes means that you'll have to permit yourself to dream.

Once I started to dream, the possibilities exploded around me. I've dreamed of changing the world for good, starting with my family, and my neighbor, and my town. I've begun to imagine better things.

But it wasn't always that way.

As a chubby nine-year-old, I dreamed of a new bike, gleaming, bright. And of course, it was red. And glowing.

I promised to God that if I got one for my birthday, I would clean it every day and always lock it up in the shed at night. I closed my eyes, and I could almost hear the echoing *clack-clack* of the playing cards on the spokes. It was chrome, shiny, and beautiful all over.

There were other childhood dreams of space travel and kissing a girl on the bus and throwing a baseball into the Grand Canyon. My head was in the clouds.

Lost somewhere between marriage, kids, career, and bills that never seemed to stop, reality put a halt to my dreaming antics. I settled for certainty and gave up on the world of wonder and imagination. Maybe that's what they call growing up, or maturity. Perhaps that's where God ends and man begins.

"I have a dream," shouted Martin Luther King Jr. in a sermon that still reverberates across the ocean of time. He saw a situation and envisioned a better day for everyone. His dream is coming true. What would have happened if he had never uttered what God had impressed on his heart?

The world is full of dreamers, and many of them become doers. They are the ones propelling us forward, moving us into the future. The doers aren't held back by the past. They are all about tomorrow.

Like a woman named Ahlaam.

Her Name Means "Dreams"

When I visited a refugee camp in Jordan, I was struck by the power of dreams.

The families lived in units called "caravans." They're little more than a series of eight-by-fifteen-feet hard-shell metal boxes each with a window. Set up like a miniature trailer park, children play and women huddle in groups while men tell stories. But for these eighty-two Iraqi refugees, this would never be home.

It should have been the place of nightmares, a place where happy aspirations of a bright future go to die. But not for one woman. Her name was Ahlaam. A person who spoke Arabic told me her name means "dreams." I gently probed about her everyday life in the caravan with her husband and three children.

It was cramped, but safely away from the threats they had left, and for that she was thankful.

She tilted her head as she recounted that fateful day in August 2015.

"We left everything behind. I assumed it would be just for a day or two or a week. I never imagined we would end up here. I never imagined we would leave forever."

The family home was in the village of Qaraqosh, near Mosul, Iraq. ISIS was at the city's edge, and the Kurds were fighting them off. Bombs from both sides often fell in their neighborhood.

One of the bombs fell near their home, killing three people, including Ahlaam's cousin. Then the Kurds withdrew, surrendering the beleaguered city to the terrorists. It was then they decided to leave.

Her children—ages fifteen, thirteen, and ten—had resumed school in the camp, and she was grateful to have that structure for them. Like any mom, she almost preened, bragging on their grades and their aptitude scores.

It was humbling for the family to live in these conditions. Ahlaam's husband was a flooring specialist in Iraq, an expert at laying ceramic tile. "We had a good life. We lived in a castle. Now, the rain comes through our roof."

Her husband had served as an interpreter for US forces in the past, and while living in Mosul, he was threatened with his life. A friend who had provided similar services was murdered.

I asked if, after all this time, she doubted God.

She shook her head. "No, my faith is getting stronger."

I asked her if she was angry at the people who scattered her eight brothers and sisters, forcing them to leave their homes.

"Jesus said, 'People will persecute you in my name,'" she said without thinking. "And he also told us to pray for our enemies. So, I pray that God will rescue all the Christians in Iraq. And I pray for Daesh [ISIS] that their hearts will change."

If this woman can dream for peace in the Middle East and for her family, then why can't you and I dream for bigger, seemingly impossible things in our lives?

Four Possibilities for Your Dreams

Whether you are dreaming of world change or a silly bicycle, there are three types of dreams: those that are *fulfilled*, those that are *delayed*, and those that are *denied*.

We all can embrace the idea of dreams *fulfilled*. But what about the others? The *delayed* dream is tough. Look at God's promise to Abraham in Genesis 15:5: "Look at the stars, Abe. Count them up. Now, look at the sand on the shore. Count them up, too. That's what your descendants will be like" (my paraphrase).

That was dreaming big. But did you know that it was a whole twenty-five years after that dream before Isaac, the second grain of sand, was born? The dream given to an old man was amazing—but then he had to wait even longer to get even a glimpse of its fulfillment.

David was selected by Samuel to be king over Israel. But there was a little problem: Israel already had a king, and Saul was his name. So David had to hide from a guy who was legitimately threatened by the lion-killing, giant-slaying young man who had won the hearts and minds of Israel. Dream *delayed*.

He wrote the Psalms from caves, never sure when the king's men would find him. He was a fugitive, hunted like a criminal. And then, one day, he was sitting on the throne. Dream *fulfilled*.

In Genesis, the brothers of Joseph have a little fun at his expense. "'Here comes that dreamer!' they said" (Genesis 37:19). Leaning on each other's shoulders, doubled over in mockery, the older brothers had quite the laugh.

Joseph had one dream which he foolishly relayed to his brothers. In their jealous cruelty, they faked his death to their father and sold him into slavery. He later landed in prison. Dream *delayed*.

Thirteen years later Joseph's dream was fulfilled when his brothers bowed their head in submission to him as their ruler, looking for a little grain to feed their families. Dream *fulfilled*.

The lad with the big ideas wasn't the popular brother. He saw things no one else could, and it caused division. And so it is with dreamers. They will never be popular. Dreamers aren't always loved. They'll be called "out of touch." They'll be scorned and talked about behind their backs. They'll lose friends. But someone around here must dream. Someone must see things the way they ought to be.

Maybe no one else will see your dream, and you'll spend your lifetime fulfilling it, alone with only God at your side. Such is the burden of a dreamer.

Of all the possibilities of dreams, the most difficult to live with are those that are dreams *denied*. We've all had God put something in our hearts, and then we spend our days denying it ever existed or making excuses why it can't be done.

What's your dream? It might be a ministry to serve poor

children, or it might be adopting one of your own. It might be a solo on Sunday morning, or it might be a chance to learn how to play the mandolin. What have you always wanted to do and never pursued?

And what excuses have you thrown up to keep you from chasing that dream? Are any of them too great for God? Just speak aloud those excuses and see how empty they are. "I'm not skilled"? He'll give you the ability. "I'm too old"? You might be wasting your skills, your wisdom, and your experience. "I'm not experienced enough"? He can cover that too.

The prophet Joel told us that in the last days "your old men will dream dreams, and your young men will see visions" (Joel 2:28 NLT).

Lie on your back and gaze at the clouds again.

It's never too late to turn the dream *denied* into the dream *fulfilled*.

What the World Needs Most

"A dream without a plan is just a fantasy." Have you ever heard this? That sounds good, but what it does is shove the dream back into the world of the impossible.

My friend Dr. Gary Davis loves the dreamer. He lives a most exciting life. By training, he is a theologian with a doctorate in cross-cultural communications. And he's also an accomplished fashion photographer. He is not afraid to take risks, to do different things, to leap into the great unknown.

He believes in living dangerously.

He asks, "What if there were no dreamers? What if we only had doers, implementers, builders, and technicians?"

And I used to have this kind of thinking thrown back at me

by logical people in my life. "Rupert, quit talking crazy." And I admit, my ideas were often a little far-fetched. I wanted to feed every hungry person, hug every lonely child, and fix every problem in every corner of the world.

Someone must cast the vision. Someone must push the boundaries. Someone must see the impossible and shake a fist at it.

Gary says, "To dream is to see beyond your present situation and to guess at what might be the next thing." He's the kind of guy who looks at Post-it Notes, Velcro, and Styrofoam, and wonders about the genius behind them.

"We need people who imagine, who think outside the box, whose perspective is so radically divergent from ours that it is hard for us to grasp. So, to the world of the pragmatists and the cautious I say, dream a little more. You have no idea what you might light upon."

I think if you dream, you shouldn't be afraid to go big. Think of all the walls that were built—or torn down—because someone had a tremendous vision. That's how we made nations, erected towering buildings, and started life-changing businesses. Someone didn't think small and ease into these things. They went big. They went bold.

John Wooden, beloved former UCLA basketball coach, said, "Make each day a masterpiece."[1] When you allow every day to grow large, you will start to step out of mediocrity into amazing.

If Not You, Then Who?

Burrowing into comfort is easy. Go to work. Come home. Tune in. Tune out.

Meanwhile, there are those who are hurting all around. And increasingly, I have to face my own selfishness.

But to be honest, it can be overwhelming.

In my closest circle of friends and family, we've seen cancer, divorce, death, suicide, and even murder. I've heard the deepest pains, the saddest sorrows, the darkest confessions.

It can be overwhelming.

I don't know how pastors do it. I don't understand how counselors sleep at night. I don't see how those who work with the impoverished move to another day.

And yet, with every person and situation that comes my way, I'm drawn deeper into their story, because that's where I'm needed.

Matthew West sings a great song called "Do Something." In the video that accompanies the song, person after person comes into view holding a sign while the music plays. The signs are simple, and yet powerful, admonitions.[2]

Adopt
Laugh
Shine
Stand up for the weak
Feed the hungry
Clean water for all
Love
Fight for Justice
Uplift
Advocate
Show Christ's Love
Comfort
Rebuild

Serve
Plant Seeds of Hope
Pray
Heal the Hurting
Volunteer
Forgive
Console the Lost
Care
Act
Stand up
Love my Neighbor
Support
Be Kind
Serve
Hug
Champion a Cause
Encourage

The lyrics of "Do Something" are equally compelling. He talks about seeing a world of trouble and struggling to make sense of why God won't intervene.

I hear that a lot. With all the pain and suffering around us, it seems like God gets an equal amount of blame for causing these troubles and for not fixing them.

And the answer comes: He created us to be the ones who make the change.

It seems we want someone else to step up, and the point of this book is that you are that someone. There is something on the tip of your heart, not put there by you but ready for this moment.

Your God Is Too Small

I took a fly-fishing lesson once. A big man (aptly named Bear) took me out to try to tame my flailing fly stroke.

According to Bear, to catch a Snake River cutthroat trout, you needed to use big, bold flies. The Double Humpy was his favorite, a massive imitation fly that is supposed to imitate, well, I don't really know what, because if I ever saw a real insect like that, I would throw my pole down and hide in the truck.

There are some who love the little midge flies, the ant patterns, or simple bugs. Not Bear. He believed in "big bugs, big fish," convinced that the largest of the cutthroats would be lured by the biggest temptation due to their immense hunger. Most other fishermen think smaller.

I think we do the same thing with our thinking. We dream little tiny dreams and act disappointed when we only get small minnows. The trophy is still in the water because we didn't even try to lure the big fish.

I read J. B. Phillips when I was a teen, and his book *Your God Is Too Small* changed my life. According to Phillips, "putting God in a box" was just an invitation for Him to ignore the limitation and do what He was going to do anyway.[3] That's good theology too. Those who try to constrain Him to dispensations or universal rules or the past are certain to be surprised.

I'm guilty of this because I like to allow some room for failure, a margin of error. I want to give myself enough room to say, "I didn't mean to say this. I meant to say that."

The truth I'm coming to find is that if I keep thinking small, it's because my faith and trust in God are too little. There's a reason child-like faith is favored. It's simple. It's uncomplicated. It's pure. It's simply saying "yes" to God without question.

I want to ask you this: When did He ever tell you to quit dreaming? When did He tell you to quit thinking big? When did He demand that you quit chasing that one thing? What caused you to give up?

The child who creates an imaginary world full of dragons and castles and princesses is much closer to almighty God than the buttoned-down theologian with a four-point sermon on the precise meaning of biblical utterances.

Dreams are God's gift to us, so quit trying to give them back to Him.

"A Man Can't Just Sit Around"

His boyhood dream was to fly. When he graduated from high school, he joined the US Air Force, hoping he would be able to pilot an airplane, but his poor eyesight was a disqualifier. He did his time and left the service, but he never abandoned his dream.

On July 2, 1982, thirty-three-year-old Larry Walters filled forty-five weather balloons with helium and tethered them to a ten-dollar Sears lawn chair. He had a bag that he filled with a liter of soda, a portable CB radio, an altimeter, and a camera.

He dubbed his flying machine Inspiration I.

He cinched a parachute to his back and gave his girlfriend a thumbs-up. Once he released the cables, he quickly found himself catapulting to the sky. In no time at all he was sailing fifteen thousand feet above the earth, floating across the Los Angeles harbor toward Long Beach.

Two airline pilots spotted him, uncertain of the flying object they could only describe as a "man floating through the sky on a lawn chair."

The terror he felt was real. All his earthly bravado was gone, floating several thousand feet below him. He was dizzy, and he was afraid he would pass out from a lack of oxygen. At three miles high, everything looked vaguely familiar and almost comforting—until he realized he was in a lawn chair.

He began to shoot the balloons one at a time with a pellet gun, hoping to gently guide his descent to the earth. But he found himself entangled in a set of lines marked "high voltage" about ten miles from his initial launch point.

He dangled from the lines, protected from electrocution by the plastic tethers. Crews eventually lowered him down by cutting power to lines, blacking out Long Beach at the same time.

In an interview not long after his flight, he was asked why he would perform such a stunt. I loved what he said. "A man can't just sit around."

He later said this to the *L.A. Times*: "It was something I had to do. I had this dream for twenty years, and if I hadn't done it, I think I would have ended up in the funny farm. I didn't think that by fulfilling my goal in life—my dream—that I would create such a stir and make people laugh."[4]

Call Me a Fool

You've heard Lawn Chair Larry's story before. His tale passed around in millions of emails, Larry was called a dunce, an idiot, and a fool. He received the very first Darwin Award. According to the society that issues the awards, the standard is lofty.

"The Darwin Award commemorates individuals who protect our gene pool by making the ultimate sacrifice of their own lives. Award winners eliminate themselves in an extraordinarily idiotic manner, thereby improving our species' chances of long-term survival."5

Those are harsh terms. And maybe that's why I love Larry. He had a dream. Sure, it defied science, common sense, and logic. But that didn't stop him from chasing it. He could have been severely injured. He could have died. But he said "yes."

For every dreamer like Larry, there are a hundred people who will stand by and criticize. Arms crossed, logic checked, reason in full display, they shake their heads in scorn. But isn't it great to surprise these doubters as we float by in our lawn chairs? We're *Living a Life of Yes*, and we're even making the city lights flicker on and off.

A few other dreamers have been called names. Noah was maybe the biggest dreamer in history and probably would have won the Darwin Award in his day. He was talking about buckets of rain in a time when the only moisture they had ever seen was a morning mist. He was talking about unfathomable amounts of water.

It wouldn't happen this week or next month or next year. It would take decades. And considering the workforce was just Noah and his immediate family, it was a long, drawn-out project.

I imagine a few disparaging names were thrown his way. And his family heard all of them too.

The dreamers are often the fools.

I have dreams—and some of them are big dreams. But I'm not sure all of them are rooted. I want to learn to play the violin. But I have never played an instrument in my life. I'll drive the neighbors crazy and inspire every cat for a mile around to head for the hills, but what's the worst that could happen?

I have dreams about travel, adventure, hobbies, and activities.

One of them is to kayak the Panama Canal. That may be the water equivalent of a floating lawn chair, but why not?

Writing this book was based on a dream. And I began to pursue it. I knew I had a story to tell—my story. But I also wanted to give voice to some of the others out there who were *Living a Life of Yes*. I asked friends and acquaintances, families, and neighbors for leads. I posted on Facebook, looking for great stories.

I was building my ark. I was going down to Sears, buying my lawn chair.

And then someone came along, this stranger on Facebook, and suggested my approach was all wrong. "I'm not a fan of formulaic writing. And your cattle call for stories will never work." Wagging his finger dipped in the well of expertise, he tried to squash my dream.

Well, I ignored him and proceeded to find story after story about amazing people.

I've found that when you ignore everyone else, it gives you a chance to listen to your heart. It gives you the opportunity to hear the voice of God that often speaks through your very mind in the stillness of the night.

The book of Psalms starts out just like this in chapter 1, verse 1.

> *"Blessed is the man who walks not in the counsel of the wicked, nor stands in the way of sinners, nor sits in the seat of scoffers" (ESV).*

These scoffers are the people who say it can't be done.

These are the people who cross their arms in disapproval.

These are the people who are just sitting around.

Once you allow yourself to dream, then you'd better be ready to *do*. You'd better be prepared to go beyond thoughts and prayers.

3

BEYOND THOUGHTS AND PRAYERS

"If you insist on saving your life, you will lose it. Only those who throw away their lives for my sake and for the sake of the Good News will ever know what it means to really live."
—*Mark 8:35 (TLB)*

The news about tragedy literally travels the globe in a matter of minutes. Social networks like Facebook and Twitter combined with television and traditional media can immediately shock the world.

A mass murder, an accident with multiple casualties, or an event that perforates our social conscience has a way of gripping all of us.

I'm addicted to TV news when something like this happens. I can't stop watching breathless reporters looking for victims and at the same time being scared half to death themselves. I can't stop watching the seesaw of shock, fear, and dismay.

We all want to do something in a crisis, but most of us feel helpless. So, we offer our thoughts and prayers.

I've done that, offered the words when I don't know anything else to say.

Of course, politicians and leaders have to say something in the face of tragedy. To tweet out "thoughts and prayers" is almost automatic these days. After tragedies, I've seen "thoughts and prayers" uttered by such diverse entities and people as the 7-Eleven corporation, Queen Elizabeth II, the Florida Marlins baseball team, and the pop star Beyoncé.

Now don't get me wrong. When we send our thoughts to the needy, to the suffering, to the hurting, they are essential. When my father died, and then my mother followed him after a short period of time, the idea that people were thinking of me was tremendously helpful. The emails, texts, cards, and letters that poured in proved to be of great comfort.

And prayers are those silent weapons that do change things. To tell someone that you are praying for them, and mean it, has marvelous influence. When tragedy hits, we turn to God, looking for an answer, looking for hope. Even the prayers of those who do not believe, who think it's a big bunch of hogwash, are welcome. Just pray. Please.

To attack a person who offers "thoughts and prayers" isn't necessary. They need to say something and offer encouragement to the rest of us.

But for me, I need to offer more. I'm at the point in my life where I'm no longer satisfied with just thoughts and prayers. If that's all I'm offering, I am no longer in the service of love, of compassion, of change. I have hung up my uniform and ceded the fight to another.

Compassion Is a Call to Action

I don't want you and others to stop thinking and praying for those who are impacted by tragedy, but I also believe there are times when we must do more.

I would never tell you to give up sending thoughts to victims of terror, or violence, or devastation. Don't quit praying for those who have been diagnosed with cancer or have lost a loved one or been fired from a job.

But in addition to thoughts and prayers, I believe we all need to add one more word: "do."

We hear stories about people in tight spots. We see them on TV or read their stories in online journals. And then we respond. We click on GoFundMe links and send a simple text message to the Red Cross. We contribute money to the church or donate our change to the plastic bucket at the hardware store. These are worthwhile and important. A dollar – or a thousand – can make a difference.

But true compassion sometimes means a call to action. And the work is rarely convenient.

When you combine compassion with mercy, then the world begins to change. When you look at policemen, firemen, nurses and doctors, and others, these are the people who run to danger.

Every year on 9/11, the anniversary of the terrorist attacks on our country rolls around. It's a date that we should never forget but all of us wish had never happened.

When the Twin Towers fell in New York City, one of the most vivid memories of that day was the image of men and women, covered in equal parts soot and tears and fear, running away from the horror of the carnage.

But running against the stream were policemen and firemen,

men and women in uniform, rushing the opposite way toward the danger of the fire, dust, and molten metal. Since that day, we have a newfound honor for these everyday heroes, holding them in high esteem.

In our society, we rightly honor those who fight the flames and rescue others from a wildfire's march. We salute those who brave rising waters to rescue the trapped and drowning. We cheer those who attend to the broken, comfort the frightened, and guide the confused.

Some responders are paid well—and they deserve every penny. But did you know that three out of four firefighters are volunteers? Around the West, with fires torching our forests every August, it's often the volunteers who are the first ones on the scene. When I compare that to my own sense of "bravado," I am ashamed.

When I see an accident on the side of the road, I might rubberneck to see what's happening, but my first instinct is not to get out of my car and render aid. When we are confronted by an issue or a problem, we often reach for a convenient excuse.

Are we first responders to pain? Do we rush to give mercy, or do we just look at the carnage and move on?

Job One: Stop the Bleeding

Every first responder has a set of protocols. Regardless if they are medical or law enforcement, if they come upon an injured person, their first job is to stop the bleeding; then they worry about everything else. If a person is bleeding, their time could be very short. Pressure or a tourniquet or another first aid technique will stop the flow.

After the bleeding stops, then others can worry about the person's healing.

And this can apply to you and me. Sometimes saying "yes" to someone is merely to help stop the one thing that is killing them, that is threatening their very existence. It might be moving someone out of a dangerous living situation. It might be helping a pregnant friend clean out her extra room to prepare for another child. It might be taking someone to their DUI class so they can get on with their life.

Find ways of being a first responder and react with a first step. It takes away the pressure of thinking you need to fix someone's entire life. Sometimes they just need some aid to deal with the pain they've inflicted upon themselves.

I've done plenty of stupid things to my body. Once, I nearly cut off my index finger with a kitchen knife while opening the stubborn plastic packaging on a kitchen gadget. In the emergency room, it seemed I had to tell the story a dozen times to nurses and medical assistants, each time feeling a little more sheepish.

But every person in there wanted to stop the bleeding. And the tender-loving emergency room doctor worked to stitch my tendons together so I could use my hand in the future to work and write these words. He had spent several years working in prison. "I saw lots of shankings in my day," he told me. "I can fix this."

He didn't predicate his care on my own intelligence or dexterity opening packages. Just because I got myself into the situation by using a knife, when a pair of scissors would have worked, didn't eliminate me from his mercy. Because I was stupid didn't mean he couldn't be compassionate.

Say "Yes" to Mercy

I have a friend who lost a great career with a promising future because he couldn't resist the lure of stealing $200. I have another friend who cheated on his wife, who was beautiful and attentive and seemingly perfect. He lost her and half of his income.

They still need my compassion. They still need my mercy.

A first responder never asks the victim what they did to cause their pain and then judges their response.

We need to say "yes" to bestowing mercy. And that alone will shock people. Extending love to the guilty, the unlovable, the shameful is entirely out of the ordinary—and a perfect place to start.

Saying "yes" to offering mercy will make people misjudge you, your intentions. Do it anyway.

As Christians, our job is to be the first responder, the person who goes straight into the situation that everyone else is leaving. We are the people who are called to reach out to stop the bleeding, to care for the wounds, to put salve on a situation.

Too often we fail to respond because we don't think we don't have the training, or the right experience, or the necessary skills. But I'm finding that God will provide exactly what we need if we just take the leap.

If there is a building with smoke billowing out the windows and there are people inside, firefighters will do everything they can to fight through the smoke and heat and fire in order to rescue the trapped.

Their only goal at that moment is to rescue.

The first responder doesn't stand with his hands on his hips berating the fool who left the stove on or judging the old woman who let her sweater stay too close to the radiator.

They risk everything because they are driven by compassion.

If they were concerned with their own comfort, safety, and ease, first responders wouldn't enter the building. In fact, they would never leave the fire station.

People who are *Living a Life of Yes* need to be ready for sacrifice. Maybe it's the ultimate sacrifice—your own life.

First responders know that when there is trouble, it is their job to rush to help and protect. They know they are putting their very lives at risk, but they do so because they are driven by a heart full of mercy.

Sometimes the pain is caused by the person. Sometimes it's caused by others. Sometimes it's caused by the natural world.

What's in Your Pile?

In 2017 devastating dual hurricanes impacted the South. Harvey would inundate Houston, and Irma would later strike Florida.

At the time, I was working in the Strategic Communications division of the US Postal Service. This job is all about managing the crisis. With hundreds of millions of customers, 600,000 employees, and 30,000 facilities, there are plenty of crises that occur. Some of them could escalate quickly and put the organization at risk. It's a challenging job with no two days alike.

When the storm first blew into the Gulf Coast, I was in Denver, far away from the rising waters and the damaging winds. In fact, we were planning on a long Labor Day camping trip. But as the water and then the wind battered the area, the demands on the local USPS staff soon became overwhelming.

They didn't ask for help—but I imagined the need was great.

And I was right. The senior officials eagerly accepted my offer to help.

I looked at the camping gear on the ready in the garage. I tried not to look at the perfect weather forecast for Twin Lakes, Colorado. I didn't look into the eyes of my dog. I kissed my wife good-bye and—with her blessing—boarded the next flight to Houston.

When I got there, the air was swampy. There was a musty smell everywhere I went. Strangely, the only thing that smelled good was the occasional front yard bonfire as people incinerated their household items before the mold set in.

Everything else was on the curb, stacked high. There was the solidarity of devastation. In some neighborhoods, no home had been spared.

It was sad to see people's possessions like this, a premature disposal of a lifetime of accumulation. These were the things they had spent their whole lives saving for. A couch from Grandma. A treasured chest of drawers. Clothes for school. Gone.

My heart was broken continuously. There was so much devastation, and I was just one man. My apathy was drowned out by the call for empathy.

I was assigned a specific role to help my organization participate in the recovery from a record rainfall that nearly washed this city into the Gulf. Each day was long, as I consulted with Postal Service leaders about how to communicate the operational impacts. I helped to communicate their actions as they calculated moving from Point A to Point B, all the while wading through scarce resources, impacted employees, and entire portions of the city still under many feet of water.

I had a team working with me and others supporting from

afar, but it was still exhausting work. There are never enough hours when lives and others' well-being depend on you. But there is still a time when the brain says "enough" and you must call it a day.

I left the command center that first night, and all I thought about was how to fill my stomach that had gone all day on a pint of yogurt and a cup of lousy hotel coffee. As I drove looking for a food spot that was open despite the devastation, I spotted two massive churches. Their neon signs were still working, and their grounds were tidy with not a hint of disaster. And not a block away were two little churches, just a few hundred feet from each other.

One was a little Cambodian Baptist Church. They had a big pile of rugs, chairs, and papers all heaped outside in the parking lot. There were chairs on the lawn and long tables with women scooping food with large spoons. The children were playing tag, and the men were planning out the task that lay ahead. It seemed the congregation had used the occasion to gather and to celebrate their unity.

And the other church was a simple building, the New Covenant Missionary Baptist Church.

I slowed down to peer into the open doors like a drive-by lookie-loo glancing into someone else's misery, hoping it wasn't so bad. It did look bad. And to make it worse, two sets of eyes caught mine before I could glance away. I sped up.

I heard the familiar voices say, "This isn't your problem. They will be okay. There are hundreds of thousands of others to help." You know the voices.

And then there was this final argument, the Evil One's trump card: "You're just one man."

That got me, catching my logic at just the right moment of

selfishness. I pulled out of the driveway and sped away. But then my mantra, my promise to God, shouted back at me. "Just say "yes"? Or is that just when it's convenient, when you're well rested, or when it suits you?"

So I flipped back, got out of the car, and walked right into the church. Those same eyes were on me right away. I probably looked like an inspector from the city or some bureaucratic troublemaker ready to "help."

But mainly I stood out because I was white. And not many men like me just wander into a black church.

The pastor, Reverend Timothy Maddox, met me after just a few moments.

I didn't waste a lot of time. "Please tell me your story and how I can help."

His uncertainty of me melted. He told me that I could just pray. And ask others to pray.

I asked about the damage. "Not too bad," Maddox said. But I could smell the water mixing with plaster and carpet. I could hear the fans blowing across the wet floor.

"We are blessed," said Pastor Maddox. I looked for insincerity, but I found none. He was counting his blessings, naming them one by one. He showed me the rooms that got it the worst —his study and the children's Sunday school room. I saw his bookshelf and the creep of the water on the pages of his trusty texts.

I asked him, "Were there books there? Did the water reach them?" He admitted that, yes, he had lost quite a few of his treasured books. His associate had lost almost all his library. And the children's Sunday school material was gone too.

Just Go There

I then decided to dive deeper. It wasn't enough for me to pretend to be a do-gooder, an emotional tourist. I needed to open up and talk about some of these broader issues with Pastor Maddox.

My friend Deidra Riggs, author of *One: Unity in a Divided World*, encourages suburban whites to venture into racial situations where we are most uncomfortable. She says this simple act will lead to discovery and life-altering interactions.[1]

And that's what led me to keep pressing in with Pastor Maddox. I blurted out, almost in a breathless sentence, that I went to a primarily white church and that my friends back home wanted to extend love to our friends in his church. I told him that we were sorry for the mess this world is in and that we have been praying for Houston. And that we would pray for him. And then I took a breath.

He looked at me and just smiled.

Deidra is right of course. Many of today's most difficult, yet needed, conversations have never been uttered because we have never taken the time to start them. They involve discomfort. And too often when we try, we make things worse.

None of this is easy for any of us, but we must "go there" to shake up our preconceptions, to destroy our inhibitions, to change our future.

After my confession, Pastor Maddox put his arm around my shoulders, and we went outside and looked at the pile of books. A soggy Bible. Stacks of literature. Books worn from study. All ruined.

I was there to do a job, helping the Postal Service restore delivery to flooded-out areas. I couldn't clean out homes. I couldn't stack furniture on the side of the road. But I could help this man and this little church.

I set up a GoFundMe page, and in just a few hours, I was able to raise enough money to help give them a reboot.

"It was a strange situation. We live in a strange world. We look for confirmation. But you walked in, and we recognized that you were a different person, being a white male. And all of us were black males. But when God is in the midst of it, the only thing that matters is mission," Pastor Maddox later told me.

Was I crazy?

"Of course not," he said. "God has always been known to do strange things."

The pastor used Jesus' first miracle turning water into wine as an example. You remember the story. He was at a wedding. He told the host to bring out six big water pots. A couple people doubted the wisdom of water; after all, people were there for the wine.

Jesus' mother, Mary, likely didn't fully understand the strangeness either. But she spoke wisdom drawn from a well she couldn't fathom. "Whatever [Jesus] says to you, do it" (John 2:5 AMP).

We need to just "do it," not for Nike's sake, but to change the world.

Jesus said that He was "the good shepherd. The good shepherd lays down his life for the sheep" (John 10:11).

This attitude of sacrifice for silly, stupid sheep should say something to us all. The sheep don't always know what it needs. It doesn't know of the danger. It doesn't know even what to ask for. But the shepherd rushes in and gives comfort.

I wasn't really the most qualified person to go to Houston or to the Middle East. There were others who had far more experience than I had. I didn't go to find glory or be a hero.

But through these situations, and the examples of others, I'm starting to see the benefit in rushing in to meet those who are suffering, in search of ways to help.

4

WHAT'S YOUR EXCUSE?

*"Now therefore go, and I will be with your mouth
and teach you what you shall speak."*
—Exodus 4:12 (ESV)

There are a thousand reasons not to do something, to keep from diving into the deep end of the pool. I get it. I've used them all.

I'm too old.

I'm too young.

The problem's too big.

I'm not qualified.

I have a family.

You might be housebound by sickness. Your finances might trip you up before you can even get out your front door. You might have a brood of little kids that need you every hour. You might have a job or a situation that keeps you from getting in a car or on an airplane.

But maybe saying "yes" isn't to a grand venture. Perhaps it's only moving forward in a smaller fashion—something that is still a stretch of faith.

I've seen people organize fundraisers, or send a care package, or gather a group of other friends who are similarly bound by a situation and resolve to do something.

If you need an excuse, you'll always find one. You don't even have to go looking. It will find you. Likely, it will have already been whispering to you, just when you teeter on the edge of decision. It will be written on the top of every page you write.

The excuse you are looking for will be voiced by your closest friends. A spouse or a confidant will raise an eyebrow or ask a question that doesn't mean to hurt, but it still burrows in, looking to infect your confidence. That one person that you thought believed in you might be the source of your deepest fear.

The excuse swirls in the wind, just when you are speaking to the sky, looking to God for help.

Do you want excuses? You can find them.

It's Uncomfortable

I love the story of the good Samaritan because it so perfectly illustrates humanity. We see the broken, busted-up, needy people, and one by one we pass them up.

Jesus told the story to illustrate an answer to the question asked in Luke 10:29 (NLV): "Who is my neighbor?" I think we are continually trying to limit our responsibility, to narrow our world and our scope. If we can narrowly define "neighbor" as those on either side of us and to the house immediately across the street, then that relieves us of loving the cranky guy on the corner. That restriction helps us ignore the single woman down the road who is pregnant for a third time with no husband in sight. It assuages our guilt about not helping the guy across town who lost another job.

I like to draw a circle and then tell God He is free to work within those limits. "I'll go where you want, as long as it's within these perfectly thought out parameters."

Jesus has a way of shaking us out of what is comfortable.

One of the women at my church said "yes," and it changed her life. Angie worked at a high-end salon in downtown Denver. It was her dream job, one she had trained for, and she worked hard to get a booth there. It was the ultimate in prestige for her profession.

One day a teenager walked into the salon. To her, he exceeded the standard scruffiness of youth. Judging by his dress and his grooming, it was apparent he was homeless. He asked to use a telephone, and she handed over her cell phone to use.

As he spoke to the other party, she was overcome with compassion. When he hung up, she told him to sit down and she would give him a shampoo and haircut. He grudgingly gave in to her infectious smile. When she finally spun him around in the chair for the big reveal in front of the mirror, his furrowed crease turned into a smile that lit the room.

"I could see a load lifted off his shoulders. Suddenly he found dignity," Angie later said.

That one haircut, that one moment of discomfort, changed the trajectory of her life. Angie was forced to leave her dream job but later opened her own studio. You see, the owners of the other place didn't take kindly to her act of compassion.

Now she can give haircuts to whomever she wants. And her heart for giving dignity to the homeless and the poor has opened her world. One unsuspecting moment that inconvenienced her has forever impacted her—and others.

"This has flipped my life upside down," she said. "You think you are changing them, but they change you."

I Feel out of Place

It was just three days after the horrific shooting in a church in Charleston, South Carolina. Nine people, open Bibles, heads bowed, seeking God. They should have been safe. They shouldn't have had to worry about murder and death. Mothers. Fathers. Sisters. And a pastor . . . gone, snuffed out by a man bent on starting a war between the races. What he didn't know is that he might have ignited a campaign of love.

What he intended for evil, God was using for good.

We sat outside the Denver Shorter African Methodist Episcopal (AME) Church. Not a single part of the long name resonated with my being or background, except "Church."

I was first moved to action after I heard the love and forgiveness given by the family of those who were killed.

"I forgive you, and my family forgives you," said Anthony Thompson, husband of shooting victim Myra Thompson. "We would like you to take this opportunity to repent. . . . Do that and you'll be better off than you are right now."[1]

What manner of love was this?

But what was a middle-aged white guy in Denver like me supposed to do? I can't fix the bigger problems in society. I can't bring sides together separated for generations.

But I can "go there" when it comes to race relations. Maybe

I couldn't go to Charleston, but the next closest thing was the AME church in Denver, whose pastor was personal friends with the slain Charleston pastor.

Admittedly, my wife and I wondered how we would be received. After all, it was a white man sitting in the middle of a prayer service who killed the Charleston nine.

There were politicians at the church, and media.

Please, God, not a sideshow, please, I thought. But from the moment we walked in, we were loved. We were welcomed and received with warmth. It was great to sit near my new friend Patricia Raybon. But even if she wasn't there, we would have felt at home.

The sermon was out of Job, and the passage focused on the words "the Lord restores." Job lost everything, and yet God restored Job with all that he'd lost . . . and more.

"We might endure for a night, but joy comes in the morning. God will restore. God will make a way. God will show up." Pastor Timothy Tyler preached with passion. He was forceful. He was emotional. And he had every right to be. He lost his friend for no reason, except to evil. "I was mad at God. I couldn't pray. I couldn't talk to Him. But people who are mad at God have great faith, because you can't be mad at someone you don't believe in."

He also spoke out against the rush to forgive. "First, we must grieve."

And grieve they did.

Sure, I felt out of place. But it never felt more right.

It's Inconvenient

When I fly on an airplane, I usually have a plan. And it doesn't involve people. I have a stack of papers, or unread papers, or magazines. Sometimes I'll bring my pile of mail. It's the perfect time to catch up.

If you are like me, having many irons in the fire means continually sorting, shuffling, and restarting. And I find I try to steal moments, and there is no better time to do this than while using public transportation.

But this *Living a Life of Yes* experience has taught me to look up from my private world and start to engage.

I was on a trip for work from Denver to Las Vegas, a short ninety-minute trip. The woman next to me was reading a book by Mark Batterson, *Chase the Lion*.[2] I had just finished a small group study on this great little book about chasing after life.

We started talking about Batterson's book, and somehow the conversation turned to this book project.

"You must speak to my son," the woman said.

She gave me his number, and a few weeks later I was able to connect with this remarkable young man.

Benjamin Lorden is a mechanical engineering student at a Colorado university. He describes himself as "Type A–Plus Personality."

"Everything has a time and a place. I like to have everything set in stone. Every step of my day is planned, and I don't like to deviate. It gives me comfort, having a design for my life."

Thank goodness for the exacting standards of our engineers! That's why bridges don't sway, roads don't sag, and products don't spontaneously combust.

"Engineering is a lifestyle for me. I get great satisfaction from creating a plan and then executing a plan."

But Benjamin's ordered world was shaken when he was visiting with his pastor who challenged him to start looking for interruptions.

"Interruptions are God at work," Benjamin's pastor told him.

So the engineering student began praying to be interrupted.

"It's a cool opportunity to invite God in," he said. "It keeps me focused on others and actually forces me to start looking for God to move. I find my mind opening to the possibilities. And it helps me to be proactive."

When he sees someone walking across a parking lot, he offers them a ride. When he sees someone in obvious need of help reaching for a product on a shelf, he rushes over to assist. When someone needs directions, he points the way.

"It's really nothing earth-shattering, but it's definitely disturbed my pattern, and I'm finding God all over the place. There are powerful little moments every single day."

His obedience really is in the small joys. He takes a few minutes with a friend. He takes a few minutes with a stranger. He takes a few minutes with his family.

"It helps me be proactive and not be so selfish."

He has even skipped class to be with a friend in need, a big deal for this overachieving student.

Benjamin gets frustrated. "I have lots of homework, and I'm swamped. And then something comes up, and I have to be jolted from my plan. I remind myself that I asked for this and God is just answering my prayer."

"As I look through the gospels, it doesn't seem that Jesus planned his miracles. They seemed to just happen while he was on his way to a place or to an event, 'as he was on his way.'"

"God isn't necessarily a god of plans. Sometimes he likes throwing a wrench in the process."

With a little hint of resignation and expectation he prays, "Lord, I give up the plan I so dearly hold onto."

Once you invite interruptions into your life, you'll begin to embrace them. They are opportunities for something different and with purpose. To have a loose plan is liberating – and even fun.

I'm Too Young

When I was a young married man, I was unusually devoted to my church for such a young person.

The church wanted to elevate me into leadership. At twenty-three years old, I was selected to be an elder in the church. I fought it, and I thought my excuse was valid. "I'm too young to be an elder." But a legitimate elder—a guy in his sixties—pulled me aside and opened his Bible, thumbing pages until he came to just the right one. "See here," he said. "Paul told Timothy, 'Let no man despise you because of your youth.' Right now, I'm Paul. You're Timothy. Now get out there."

From that moment I took off. I went forth with confidence, and that bred trust. I found myself leading community groups, Scout troops, church projects, and work initiatives—all before I was thirty. I wasn't overly gifted. I was just willing to jump in, despite my age.

The prophet Jeremiah struggled with a similar perception of his youth.

"But the LORD said to me, 'Do not say, "I am only a youth"; for to all to whom I send you, you shall go, and whatever I command you, you shall speak. Do not be afraid of them, for I am with you to deliver you, declares the LORD'" (Jeremiah 1:7–8 ESV).

I read about three nine-year-old classmates in northern Ohio who wanted to find a way to help the victims of Hurricane Harvey. At first, according to their teacher, Stephanie Skolosh, they asked the obvious question.

"What can we do? We're little. And we're here, far away from them."[3]

Stephanie said she "talked about praying for them."

But the St. Paul Catholic School students kept on probing. The girls decided to put up a lemonade stand to raise money for the victims in Texas. The stand had a sign: "When life gives you lemons, make lemonade."

In one day, they raised $1,000.

One of the parents said, "I think that they're big thinkers, and that's amazing as parents to see our kids as big thinkers, to be able to help other people."

Thinking big means thinking beyond who you are—or who you aren't. It means to not be dissuaded by circumstance or failures. It means not looking at all the barriers.

I'm Too Old

On the opposite side of the spectrum is age. Somehow, the last thirty years have slipped away from me. I wanted to make a big splash in life, but then I had kids. And like many married couples, we didn't have a lot of money. And then we had to make moves for work. You know, life happened.

I blinked, and midlife passed me by, and I found myself on the downside of the life calendar.

Suddenly those big life-changing projects seemed out of touch.

And I'm not alone.

Technology has a way of making you feel old. The buttons get smaller. The menus aren't intuitive. The lights start moving a little too fast. And then it hits you like a rock. Life is passing you by.

But we can't buy into that.

Life is full of world changers that got the itch, the passion, late in life.

Acclaimed writer and friend Patricia Raybon's husband, Dan, has been fighting serious illness, but he's pressing on with some life goals. He published his first book at the age of seventy. And she publicly praised this moment, extolling his accomplishment. "It's never too late," she wrote on her blog. "To grind. To fight. To struggle. To run. To create. To fall. To get back up. To keep going. To be, finally, your best."[4]

We think we are too old, too used, too weighted down.

No. Never.

I was recently introduced to Harold Patterson, and it didn't take long before he became one of my heroes.

Harold spent much of his life as an auto mechanic, fixing cars and trucks in East Texas. After he retired, he was still busy with projects and volunteer work. A friend talked him into going on a disaster relief team into Kenya.

While there, he watched members of the team spend hours with a hand drill, only to get stopped by a large rock five feet below the surface. He knew there had to be a better way.

This auto mechanic recalled his days as a youth working in the Texas oil patch. His mind went to work when he went home, and he found a way to miniaturize an oil drill.

He designed it, machined it, and has applied for a patent. The entire drill fits into a five-foot-by-three-foot crate and weighs just 1,250 pounds. It's not meant to drill just once, as it can drill several wells before the five-and-a-half-horsepower engine will give out and need to be replaced.

At seventy-three years old, why is he still doing it?

"There's still a great need," he said. "And I have the answer."

With 1.9 billion people who have very little water, bad water, or no water, there is a direct human impact to his vision.

"Mission groups go to these countries with news of the gospel," said Harold. "But they first ask for clean water to save them."

To date, Harold's team has drilled wells in Nigeria, El Salvador, Panama, Zambia, India, Haiti, Sierra Leone, the Philippines, , the Congo, Sri Lanka, Mexico, and Liberia.. Others have rallied around the vision and are providing a whole host of other services to these areas, such as food preservation, hygiene training, and school material for children.

All of this because a man in his late sixties said "yes" to a mission trip.

His organization also built and sent two thousand water filtration systems to Puerto Rico and the US Virgin Islands after the 2017 hurricanes, allowing for clean water for millions.

"You never say no!" he told me.

Just a couple years ago, Harold and his wife lost their son, Will, to an accident in a construction area while he was working on a Texas highway. As a welder, Will had been involved with building the drills from the very beginning.

In his honor, the drill is now called the WILL Drill—Water Is Lasting Life.

"I take my son with me everywhere I go," said Harold.

Since his retirement, he's been involved with more than 20 disaster response teams.

To those who think they are too old, that their days of effectiveness have passed them by, Harold has a message: Don't give up.

The world needs your knowledge, your wisdom, and your experience. No one else has walked your same path. "I only started finding my purpose after I retired, and I started saying yes. Don't let your age limit what you can do."

Maybe physical limitations will hold you back. When I spoke to Harold, he was getting ready for a shoulder operation (so he could get prepared to go to Kenya next year). That happens. But don't let that keep you from doing what you can with what you have in order to change the world.

Too old? Never. "Not as long as I have breath," said Harold.

I am a big believer in the power of curiosity. Look at Benjamin Franklin. Flying kites and starting libraries and volunteer fire stations. He started the nation's postal system, invented the cast iron stove, and even created a form of a catheter.

His mind was full of life.

In a *USA Today* article titled "A Curious Retiree Is a Happy Retiree," financial consultant Mitch Anthony concluded, "If you wake up on day 43 of retirement and realize you have no reason to get out of bed, you are in trouble." You need "a reason for waking, a purpose."[5]

If you live a life of "yes," then the curiosity of not knowing what's next in life is what drives you. It will keep you young and engaged. And you just might change the world along the way. Like Harold.

I'm Not Ready

You might be holding back, thinking you need to get your act together. You need to get ready. But the problem is that if you wait until you're ready, you'll be waiting forever. You'll never be ready.

Henry James wrote a short book called *The Madonna of the Future*. It is about a failed artist named Theobald who sees a beautiful woman and is inspired to paint her as a Madonna.[6]

He begins to study the work of others so he can paint her with perfection. But he waits so long and studies so in depth that the model grows "coarse" and "stout."

The artist dies, leaving behind a blank canvas.

I think of all the reasons that I don't say "yes," and this feeling that I cannot make a difference rings the loudest. I might have a great idea, a passion to right the wrongs.

What could I possibly do? Who I am to think that I could make a difference?

That kind of risk aversion is precisely the tool that Satan uses against Christians. We have been promised everything—wisdom, resources, and a "great cloud of witnesses" that will support us (Hebrews 12:1). Still, we listen. We waiver. We wait. We quit.

Brené Brown has this to say: "When we spend our lives waiting until we're perfect or bulletproof before we walk into the arena, we ultimately sacrifice relationships and opportunities that may not be recoverable, we squander our precious time, and we turn our backs on our gifts, those unique contributions that only we can make. Perfect and bulletproof are seductive, but they don't exist in the human experience."[7]

In other words, if you wait until you have everything

together before you act, you'll never act. If you wait until you have enough money or the time or the energy, you'll never jump. And that is the time you'll never get back. Those are opportunities you'll never get back. Your ship might just sail past you.

I Can't Stand Against the Evil

I met Anna Carroll in Jordan. She, too, was one of those surprised bloggers who was picked to tell the world the story of the other Holy Land.

And like me, she wasn't necessarily a candidate to be in the Middle East. When I met her, she was heading a ministry in Costa Rica—a world away from ISIS and refugees.

Anna grew up in a family and in a church that valued missions. She took many of her school breaks and summer vacations in Romania, Brazil, and Central America.

"My home church, where my dad was a pastor, is big into community building with missions," she told me. "We went to the same towns and villages year after year, helping them for the long haul."

As she moved out on her own, she found success as a medical assistant and thought that a career in medicine was her life's calling.

But then her heart began calling her to Costa Rica, a place she had been three times prior.

It wasn't enough just to take a two- or four-week trip and come home and show everyone a slide show.

"I felt God telling me not only to go but to sell everything and go."

She committed to six months. And a few of her friends thought she would be home in less.

"They didn't think I would make it much past that."

She spent those months at a small ministry in a low-income area, teaching at-risk children English. And sure enough, at the end of her commitment, she was making plans to return home.

Along with some friends, she went on a tourist trip to see some parts of the country that she hadn't explored yet. They ventured close to the Nicaraguan border.

"I saw little girls selling gum, and I thought nothing of it. But what I learned is that those girls were selling more than gum."

She stumbled onto a child trafficking hub, with girls as young as twelve working the border as prostitutes.

"I had no idea this was going on."

Anna had been surrounded by mission ministries long enough and presumed someone was reaching out to these girls.

"There's a ministry for everything here. Costa Rica is not an impoverished nation. So, I asked who was reaching out to them, who was ministering to them," she said.

Her friend told her that no one was working with these children and women in that specific region.

"There was no one helping them, no ministry presence at all," she said. "And there was no hashtag, no support."

She went back to her mission and started making plans for her return to the States. "But I couldn't get their faces out of my head. It wasn't guilt. I just saw the need."

After a week, Anna told me she "surrendered to the joy." The joy of saying "yes."

She admitted she didn't know what to do. But she had to do something. She met another girl in the country who happened to be from her same hometown in Kentucky. And the two young girls—Suzanna and Anna—decided to do something to stop child sex trafficking in Central America.

Once the two were on the border, they needed to establish their credibility.

So they threw a Christmas party on the border. They invited the girls, military patrols, and police from both Nicaragua and Costa Rica, and it was a huge success.

They didn't fully understand the criminal element that ran the prostitutes and the commercial sex tourism money that helped fund it.

"Taking on the criminal underworld wasn't really what we intended to do. We just wanted to reach these girls."

She admits that "naivete was actually a blessing. It was our armor. We didn't put ourselves in danger, but not knowing everything was a blessing. It allowed us to trust God for the results."

Anna admits that if she had known everything going in, she wouldn't have ventured.

Through her eight years of work there, and counting, they have been able to educate and minister to hundreds of girls.

One of the discoveries the team found is that the prostitution was generational. Babies of prostitutes grew up on the "family business" and were forced either by pimps or poverty to follow their mother's footsteps.

Lightforce, Anna and Suzanna's ministry, developed educational material and with some persistence now teaches school children about their rights and their opportunities. "We want to stop human trafficking before it starts," said Anna.

One of the little boys who was first influenced by Lightforce education is now one of the leaders, helping his younger peers from becoming vulnerable to trafficking.

In a fantastic twist of providence, Lightforce's model of prevention through early education has been duplicated in Jordan to help Syrian refugee children who have been increasingly vulnerable to similar exploitation. The materials have now been translated into Arabic and are being used throughout the region.

One young woman, who took on a huge problem, has impacted more than a thousand children and countless lives.

What Can I Possibly Do?

Maybe when you are confronted with an opportunity, you just don't know what to do. You hold back from saying "yes" because you don't know what to say or where to go. I felt that way with the Middle East. The persecution of Christians by ISIS gripped the world. Nations froze, afraid to insult Islam and yet still outraged by those who were misusing the name of Allah.

If the combined power and wisdom of the European Union, Arab States, United Nations, and the United States couldn't fix the problem, what in the world was I going to do?

I never meant to be in a fight, let alone in one playing out across the world. But this one has crossed the ocean, jumped the divide, and struck a chord right in the heartland of America. I wanted to spend the rest of my days writing about thoughtful pursuits, faith, and hope. I wanted to be a man of peace who would age gracefully, allowing the gray hair to take over my head one strand at a time.

By providence, by divine selection, by forces way out of my control, I found myself fully engaged in a world I never imagined.

I read the headlines. I turned my head when I saw the men

kneeling on the shores of Tripoli, declaring their faith even as the life was draining from their faces. I hashtagged and prayed for the hundreds of innocent Nigerian girls snatched from their school, pretending they were in a good place, hiding in the forest.

I chalked the fighting up to civil war or politics gone astray. Consumed with work, and summer vacation plans, and a car with an overdue oil change, I went about my life. After all, it wasn't my fight.

Here's the truth. I could no longer look away. ISIS-ISIL-Daesh rolled through countries like Iraq and Syria, but also Ethiopia, Nigeria, and Tunisia. They found villages that are predominantly Christian or Shia Muslim. They overran the local populace and often beheaded the men. They took the women as sex prizes and captured the children—boys and girls—to be sold as slaves. This is not crazy-eyed fundamentalist talk. This is real.

At the time, I wrote these words: "Our government wants us to believe the battle of the day is against climate change, or police power, or those who make too much money. I cannot utter one more word about such things when the rest of the world is gripped by fear."

I couldn't rely on politics, on the UN or some other power, to make a change. The cry was for humanity, and this was our call. I decided at that moment that my passion couldn't be college football, the latest smartphone, or my workout routine.

I decided to take a stand. And if I had to stand alone, then so be it.

So yes, you can say "yes." You can do something which might just lead you to something else which will eventually help you find your place. Don't think too hard about the chessboard. Just move your piece and trust God to guide you to the end.

I Have a Family

At one point in my life, I felt compelled to go to seminary. I don't know if it was a calling, but I toyed with the idea for the better part of a year. Every time I felt close, I was pulled back to the reality of two preschoolers and a wife at home. I was too practical to be obedient. I had many people tell me to have more faith, to trust God for the money.

I was raised by a one-truck roofer and a stay-at-home mother. Money always came in sporadically. "Around here, it's either chicken or feathers," my mom would say. And I saw it. During the summer when the weather was oppressive and the days long, Dad wouldn't come home until after 10:00 p.m., asphalt clinging to his clothes and the dust of the day cracking his lips. And in winter when the roofs were buried deep, he would wait for the leak, which he would go patch for fifty dollars.

I vowed never to be that trusting and dependent. I wanted a steady job and pay. I never sought independence in employment, the entrepreneurial spirit having gone to my brother instead. I wanted to know that a check was going to be in the bank every two weeks, even if it was a little less.

But that trust in an employer unfortunately led to a lack of trust in God.

I never went to seminary. And there have been many times when I've wondered what life would have been like.

The truth is my family would have relished the life. The ministry life would have been a perfect fit for my gregarious and outgoing nature. But my fear—and excuse—surrounding having family responsibilities kept me from chasing the dream.

The challenge that young families face these days is huge.

The pressures that come with having small children are real. Some are brought on by societal peer pressure. Others come from standards and requirements by schools, churches, and organizations. Life is not easy. And every commitment needs to be put through the funnel of the clock with drops of mere hours or minutes left over.

Maybe your "yes" starts with those few chronological leftovers. You can involve your children and your spouse in those moments. You can still say "yes."

Can Someone Else Be in Charge?

Have you ever been part of a team where no one will step up and take charge? Everyone looks around, hoping, praying that someone, anyone else will be responsible. You're tired of volunteering to bake the cookies, to organize the parent list, to clean up. You're always the one to host the family reunion, to load the presentation into the computer, to shovel the walks? Please, can someone else be in charge?

We cling to the wall, hiding our ability. We know full well that we could be part of the solution, and instead, by our passivity, we become part of the problem. We all have our excuses. I've used every one of them. "I'm too busy." "I don't have the right skills." "It's not the right time." "I don't have the experience." "I'm too young." "I'm too old."

I've been there. I shirk for a while, pretend to be too busy, and flick on the television or sit in the backyard thumbing through magazines, or I play a game on my phone. "There," I think. "Now I'm in control of my time."

But it doesn't take long before this mindless life works

against me. I'm not refreshed. I'm *not* more at ease. I'm miserable.

Shake off the excuses and the things that hold you back, which may involve more than mere excuses. It may be your own past keeping you from a more fulfilling present and future, which we'll explore in the next chapter.

5

MOVING BEYOND YESTERDAY

"The next time Satan reminds you of your past, remind him of his future." —Greg Laurie

So maybe you think you don't have what it takes. You are underqualified to do the job. You have a checkered past, full of problems. Me too. At times I've been a horrible person, a bad dad, a wavering husband, an unfaithful friend. I didn't live the faith I proclaimed. I was—and often am—a hypocrite.

I've been entirely unlikable, untrue, and untrustworthy.

And still, God trusted me.

Shake Off the Past

Think about the story of David in the Bible. Here was a man so full of potential. He was gifted from an early age and given every opportunity to excel.

God inserted David as king over the people of Israel, unseating Saul. David was surrounded by the "mighty men"—a group of loyal friends who would go to war to defend him. He had a best friend, Jonathan. The people shouted his name in the streets.

He had everything. Except for Bathsheba.

From his castle vantage point, he saw a flash of flesh, a woman bathing herself. Rather than look away, he peered down, watching her form. And the image wouldn't leave his mind.

The picture of Bathsheba gripped him, and then he hatched a plan. He would find a way to take her. But there was a problem. Her husband, Uriah, was also one of David's mighty men, a warrior, a leader of men, a confidant.

David slept with Bathsheba and then, to his horror, found out she was pregnant.

Compounding his problems, he decided he would have Uriah killed, purposefully pushing him to the front lines of the battle.

Sleeping with your friend's wife and then knocking him off must be among the sleaziest of crimes. That should have disqualified David in front of the people and most of all before the God he claimed to represent.

There were consequences—a heavy price to pay. The baby Bathsheba was carrying died. His reputation was sullied. His leadership suffered.

But he repented. Psalm 51 is his lament and his penitent prayer. He cried, "Have mercy on me, O God, . . . Wash away all my iniquity . . . Create in me a pure heart" (Psalm 51:1–10).

He pulled himself together and decided that he would fulfill his mission.

He said "yes" despite his terrible past.

LIVING A LIFE OF YES

We Idolize Our Scars

Maybe you're struggling to say "yes" because of your past. It's too painful, too ugly, too shameful.

I have a friend who fell off a roof in a horrific construction accident. He lost the use of the lower half of his body. But he resolved to pursue everything he had ever desired. He figured it out. He went on to get married. He continued his construction career, learning how to manage projects instead of swing hammers. He lives in rural Wyoming and drives a snowplow to clear his driveway and brings in firewood and even skis with a unique contraption. I've even been hunting with him on a four-wheeler.

His past doesn't define him.

I was recently reminded of a story about holding on to old perceptions.

In the past, when the circus still had performing elephants, they walked in meek compliance. If the trainer wanted to keep them in a specific area, they would tie them to a pole with a weak rope and walk away. These massive creatures could break just about anything humans could engineer. Why didn't they just run?

This was accomplished through careful training. The trainer secured the baby elephant with heavy chains. Every time the little guy tried to wander away, he was violently pulled back since he didn't have the physical strength to break the chain. After a few futile tugs, he simply quit in frustration. It didn't take long, and eventually he gave up even trying. He just gave in.

As the elephant grew older, the chain was replaced by a

simple, cheap rope. And the elephant never bothered testing the strength of the rope because the desire to run was gone.

Isn't that just like us? We are held captive by our past, by the limitations we once had. When they define us, they hold us back. We become our own limitation.

You probably have some history you are carrying around, things that bring you shame. Someone said something to you or did something to you. Maybe as a child you were told you were dumb, or you couldn't sing, or you were ugly. Perhaps a parent crushed your enthusiasm or a trusted elder took advantage of you. Maybe you had a significant illness. Maybe your heart was broken.

Maybe it was an act you wish you had never committed. A theft. A deception. A fateful decision.

And the result is you never tug at the rope that holds you back. If you did, it would break and you would be free. Free to pursue your dreams. Free to pursue your future. Free to pursue God's best for you.

What is most interesting is that we prop up these past injuries; we give them prominence. We idolize them. We are broken, abused, hurt. And that label becomes who we are and what we worship. These labels are often rooted in the past—old animosities carried like a beat-up Samsonite. But that's where they should stay.

In 2 Corinthians 12:9 (ESV), Paul had this to say about our weaknesses: "But he said to me, 'My grace is sufficient for you, for my power is made perfect in weakness.' Therefore, I will boast all the more gladly of my weaknesses, so that the power of Christ may rest upon me. For the sake of Christ, then, I am content with weaknesses, insults, hardships, persecutions, and calamities. For when I am weak, then I am strong."

You have things in your past—things that cause you to stutter, to pause in your pursuit of calling. Some of them were your own fault. Some of you have had shame heaped on you by others. You don't deserve the title you wear, the humiliation you bear, the sadness that never goes away.

And still, regardless of the source of your shame, God looks at you—beloved, talented, perfect.

So who are you to question His judgment?

The Secret Life of Shame

We kill our life of adventure when we allow shame, from any source, to have power over us.

Shame is that terrible, private feeling that something is wrong with us—that we are somehow defective as a person. That we are irreparably damaged. That if anyone really knew what we were like, we would be rejected.

Curt Thompson wrote these words in his book *The Soul of Shame*: "The most powerful thing that shame does is truncate our power to create."[1]

Your feelings of guilt and shame are part of your story. But all of them can be part of your victory.

In Luke 13, Jesus was teaching in one of the synagogues on the Sabbath.

> *"And, behold, there was a woman which had a spirit of infirmity eighteen years, and was bowed together, and could in no wise lift up herself"* (Luke 13:11 KJV).

Think of this woman. Some of her infirmity was physical, no doubt caused by a physical condition.

Some of it was emotional, having endured the mental anguish of eighteen years of walking stooped over.

Some of it was just a broken spirit.

If you can't stand straight, then before long, you'll just gaze at the ground and figure that's your destiny.

There are some of you who are reading this, and you are stooped from the burden of your shame. You feel like a failure. You feel like no one cares. You feel like giving up.

When Jesus hung on the cross, he was naked, bloodied, humiliated before the entire world. The sign hung above his head—King—it was meant to mock him.

He should have felt shame: after all, he was exposed; plus, he had all our sins on his back. And yet, we are told in Hebrews 12:2 that "he endured the cross, scorning its shame."

In other words, he took the sins of the world—the sins you committed and the sins committed against you—and he bore them on the cross, on his body.

And yet, he scorned the shame.

Friends, the shame is over. That dark shadow that has plagued you for years is over and done.

> "And when Jesus saw her, he called her to him, and said unto her, Woman, thou art loosed from thine infirmity. And he laid his hands on her: and immediately she was made straight, and glorified God" (Luke 13:12–13 KJV).

Friend. Be free! You are not to feel the power of failure of shame one more minute.

Stand up, and start *Living a Life of Yes*.

And there is a difference between guilt and shame.

Guilt focuses on behavior. Shame focuses on self.

Guilt says, "I did something bad." Shame says, "I am bad."

You might be holding back from saying "yes" because of the corrosive, destructive effect of shame. But it has no place in your life. If you feel guilty about something, make it right and then press on into the person God has created you to be.

Don't let shame hold you back. Stand up. Say "yes"!

And somewhere, living in that new place, you might just stumble into what you were meant to do all along. You might just make an impact that is shockingly beautiful to an ugly world. You might find yourself in a fertile field, where your actions can produce an abundant harvest. You might find people who have a story to tell—and you are the one to tell it.

Getting Rid of Our Labels

There is no greater excuse than the past, the dark shadow of yesterday that darkens the future. So many times, I've prevented myself from taking chances because of who I thought I was—or wasn't.

Those labels that I cut out and put on myself. Like going to a company dinner and filling out a name tag. "Hello, my name is_____."

I would fill out the tag with the absolute worst thing I could imagine, figuring that's who I was and who I was going to be the rest of my life.

You've been there too, right?

Remember the story Jesus told about the talents?

One servant was given five talents—probably portions of

money, measured out. You can apply this however you want. Money. Gifts. Opportunities. God has given you something.

Well, this first servant doubled what he was given, investing and making five more. Another was given two talents. He, too, invested and made two more.

The master in the story said this: "You have been faithful over a little; I will set you over much. Enter into the joy of your master" (Matthew 25:23 ESV).

What a beautiful story about using what God has given you. Both the five-talent guy and the two-talent guy entered into the joy of the master. That's a beautiful place when you have said "yes" and you are blessed.

This book is full of stories of people who are walking in that joy.

But what happened to the one-talent guy?

He said this to the master: "So I was afraid and went out and hid your gold in the ground. See, here is what belongs to you" (Matthew 25:25).

Sound familiar?

There are two-talent people reading these words. Five-talent people too. And ten-talent people. And there's a bunch of us with just one talent.

You might be thinking, "Who am I?"

"I'm a blue-collar worker who works with his hands."

"I'm a housewife and a mother."

"I'm retired, too old for anyone to listen to my words."

"I'm too young. I just don't have the experience needed."

We take that one talent, and we hide it because we don't think it's much.

What an insult to the Master who gave you that gift in the first place.

So much of this talent waste is tied to our past—those ancient memories from yesterday that keep you from a new tomorrow.

If you are like me, you carry around a degree of an inferiority complex. You don't have a tremendous pedigree or a long list of accomplishments. Your close friends can be named on one hand. Your words and actions are rarely noticed. But let me encourage you to surrender to His story.

The book of Acts records some of the most amazing days in all of human history.

I love this verse in Acts 4:13: "When they saw the courage of Peter and John and realized that they were unschooled, ordinary men, they were astonished and they took note that these men had been with Jesus."

They overcome their limitations, and with boldness they spoke to a hostile audience. And because they said "yes," they helped tell the story that has impacted billions of lives since.

History is filled with men and women who stepped out of their past into glorious futures. They were simple. They were flawed. They were imperfect.

There are others who gave up, who listened to the lies about their lives. We don't know their names, and they are likely lost to anonymity.

I'm not ready to give up. And I don't think you are either.

6

OVERCOME THE FEAR

"There is only one way to avoid criticism: do nothing, say nothing, and be nothing." —Aristotle

So many of the reasons we don't leap are rooted in fear, aren't they?

If we fail, we'll lose prestige. We'll lose money. We'll lose friends.

We're afraid we'll lose out on life and our comfort, peace, and stability. We are worried that we'll lose out on some of these things—maybe all of them.

Fear is one of those fascinating emotions that has psychological, physiological, and emotional roots.

Psychologists tell us that we are born with only two fears: falling and loud noises. Babies have no other built-in fear. They learn every other anxiety by experience, a learned ability to survive.

Although that's part of growing up, fear can also be a disability. Most of our worries about the future come from our past.

Let's have an open talk about fear.

What's Everyone Thinking?

One of the biggest hindrances to a life unleashed is the fear of others. We fear what they will think of us.

The Bible calls this the "fear of man" (Proverbs 29:25).

Deep inside nearly every heart is this fear. It comes alive especially at the start of a venture because everything is fragile, new, and untested.

It's interesting because so many start these undertakings with such vigor and enthusiasm. "Get out of my way. I have a vision, I have a purpose, I have a goal!"

But then comes a single criticism, often from a person who really doesn't have a say in the matter. They haven't earned the right to speak into the situation, and yet they do.

I have one relative who stands in opposition to what I do. Some of it is personality driven. Some of it is philosophy. But for whatever reason, I dwell on every criticism this person lobs my way. I ruminate on the words, rolling them over in my head hour by hour as I wrestle in my sleep.

Every new venture I take, I know, will be met with opposition by this person. And I find myself purposefully trying to mitigate and maneuver my efforts so they cannot criticize.

Meanwhile, my vision suffers because I'm striving to please this one person.

Teddy Roosevelt gave a speech more than a hundred years ago. He had more than his share of critics. And he answered their pointed barbs in just a few sentences:

It is not the critic who counts; not the man who points out how the strong man stumbles, or where the doer of deeds could have done them better. The credit belongs to the man who is actually in the arena, whose face is marred by dust and sweat and blood; who strives valiantly; who errs, who comes short again and again, because there is no effort without error and shortcoming; but who does actually strive to do the deeds; who knows great enthusiasms, the great devotions; who spends himself in a worthy cause; who at the best knows in the end the triumph of high achievement, and who at the worst, if he fails, at least fails while daring greatly.

We've all suffered at the hands of those who throw words carelessly. Online social media is a particularly fierce place and not for the tender heart.

I'm trying to put the critics in my life in proper perspective.

You Will Not Please Everyone

I am always amazed at the fearlessness of Peter. After his denial of Jesus, he went on to become the rock of the church. He boldly spoke before Roman and Jewish leaders alike. He was unflappable, unstoppable.

But then there is this curious passage in Galatians 2. Paul is writing, and he talks about having "a face-to-face confrontation with [Peter] because he was clearly out of line" (Galatians 2:11 MSG).

The situation was that Peter regularly ate with non-Jews—the Greeks and pagans who had converted to Christ. But when the pious Jewish converts came to town, he was a different man. He was playing both sides because he was afraid of what they thought.

Paul called it a "charade."

I am guilty of this very thing. For years, I tried too hard to "become all things to all people" (1 Corinthians 9:22). I wanted to appeal to the young and to the old. I wanted to be viewed as holy to the church and as acceptable to the unchurched. I tried to look mature and yet youthful. I wanted to be handsome and yet common.

I abused the intent of this scripture, and in the process lost all my impact. I spent so much time trying to appeal to everyone that I appealed to no one.

Brené Brown says this: "I carry a small sheet of paper in my wallet that has written on it the names of people whose opinions of me matter. To be on that list, you have to love me for my strengths and struggles." [1]

God's Word and the call on your life must loom more significant than the words of people.

Don't Wait for the Masses to Cheer

The truth is if you are on the right track, there will never be 100 percent approval.

When you say "yes," I can almost guarantee that there will be someone who will say "no."

Some of it is the law of averages. In every crowd, there's the one person who feels they must speak their mind. These people really believe they are deliverers of truth, and they take great pride in speaking without filters. I have found that they are often just rude, using truth-telling as an excuse for their own insensitive behavior.

Still, we want our parents, our family, our friends, and our coworkers to agree with our every plan. We yearn for their approval, for their applause. Post a photo or something profound on Facebook, and if you are like me, you desperately check to make sure it's seen and given a thumbs-up by everyone who matters most. We want likes and shares. We secretly want applause and a pat on the back. We want a good word.

But this dependence on approval from others distracts us from our calling. So when someone says "no," it matters too much.

Don't let the naysayer steal your joy. Don't let that one negative person throw water on your zeal, quenching your fire. Once you throw off this dependence on the opinions of others, you'll find your confidence to move forward.

In Mark chapter 11, the crowd was cheering for Jesus. They laid down palms and shouted "Hosanna." In chapter 15 the crowd was screaming for Barabbas to be released and Jesus to be hung on a cross. If the crowd turned on Jesus, who knew no sin, what do you think they'll do to you?

Forget the crowd.

If you are waiting for everyone to support your effort, let me give you a reality check. There will be doubters. There will be some who will reject you.

But God has given you exactly what you need. And what a shame that rejection from a single person has a way of undoing all of creation. It shouldn't be that way.

Permission to Tremble

We sometimes feel guilty about our fear, equating it with weak character or faith. But the Bible is full of stories of fear, even among those who knew Jesus best.

He was birthed into a time of great fear. Mary was told to

quit fearing. Another angel told Joseph to not be afraid. A violent ruler later forced them to flee their home.

The disciples were marked by fear. When Jesus calmed a storm, the disciples "were terrified" (Matthew 14:26). When they saw him walking on water, they felt the same: "'It's a ghost,' they said, and cried out in fear" (Matthew 14:26). They eventually scattered at the Crucifixion—out of fear.

A recent Chapman University study on fear broke down our personal fear into different categories.[2]

The first category was born out of **safety**. It included accidents, future financial stability, identity theft and privacy concerns, and criminal victimization.

The second category centered on concerns for the **physical world** around us, including the effects of pollution, global warming, asteroid strikes, earthquakes, and volcanoes. It also included fear of floods, hurricanes, and terrorist attacks.

When you look at this list, fear doesn't seem to be such a bad thing. Tidal waves? Sharks? Government overreach? Nuclear war? All are valid concerns.

Fear is good and useful. A perfectly legitimate preservation tool. A healthy attitude toward fear is to keep it at bay without yielding our emotions to it.

Think about the last time you were startled or even frightened by an unexpected noise.

One hot August night, my wife and I were sleeping with the sliding glass door open. We were jolted from our first hour of sleep by a slow, scraping sound against the side of the house, and then a thump. And then we saw a motion light triggered in the backyard.

Immediately my physical fear instinct kicked in. I felt my heart beat quicker. My throat got a little tighter. The hair on my neck stood straight out as my skin tensed. The adrenaline pumped through my body, and suddenly my emotions began to react. Should I go out and inspect? And if I do, am I ready to fight? Should I just lock the door? Should I call 911?

I pulled on some pants and slipped on some shoes and inched my way outside, my fists clenched, ready for anything. My eyes adjusting to the limited light, I looked for the intruder. I searched the entire yard, the shrubbery, and the shed. Eventually I found the culprit: a shovel, leaned against the house earlier in the day, had decided at precisely 11:21 p.m. to fall to the ground.

I picked up the shovel with both arms and marched into the house, both hands gripping the neck in a victorious submission hold.

Fear can be reasonable and helpful. That's why we flinch at the flame, duck at the swinging branch, and swerve at the parked car in our lane. But it can also be unreasonable. God gave us fear to serve us—not govern us. It's a tool to keep us safe, to keep us close to him, and to keep us alert.

The last category of fears from the Chapman study are probably the ones you and I deal with most of the time: **personal**, such as safety in different spaces, anxiety about one's future, and phobias.

I can understand that going to a foreign, third-world country carries its own set of fears. Do I really need to list them? Bugs. Bad water. Terrorism. Different food. Some of you will add to this list quite readily.

What fears are holding you back from *Living a Life of Yes*? When you say "no," you are probably tying your response to a few specific fears. Some are general. Some are very pointed.

Most of us spend our lives running from that which we fear.

We forgo all the things we could experience simply because of the unknown. We let fear become our god.

There is value in naming the fear. Write it down. Share it with friends. Either that fear will be found to be legitimate, or you'll realize it's unreasonable and walk past it toward your calling.

The Fear of Looking Foolish

Do you remember the one time you raised your hand in class and the other kids snickered?

Or that one time when you sang too loud or a little off-key?

Or when you walked in late to an event and the only seat was in the front, and you stumbled in front of everyone?

Or when the mustard escaped the hot dog bun onto your shirt?

It seems unless you have lived the charmed life, there will be moments of "glory" that remind the world that you are human.

I remember spending a day visiting with people at a conference where I was speaking. I had dinner and then addressed the crowd on a stage with a wireless microphone and no lectern. My surprise came after the last handshake, realizing that my zipper had been down the entire evening. Mr. Has-All-the-Answers can't even pull up his fly. Yup, that's me.

I had a man come up to me afterward and pour his life and his heart out, repeating back my words and how much they meant to him. Never even noticed the zipper.

Mark Batterson, in his book *Chase the Lion*, gives an excellent summary of fools in the Bible: "Noah looked foolish building an ark in the desert. Sarah looked foolish buying maternity clothes at age ninety. David looked foolish attacking Goliath with a slingshot."[3]

That's quite a list!

And he continues, "The wise men looked foolish following a star. Peter looked foolish stepping out of the boat. Jesus looked foolish hanging half naked on the cross."[4]

"Faith is the willingness to look foolish."[5] In fact, that might just be the definition of faith itself.

The Bible is full of warnings for the fool. Paul often turns things around, making ironic references. He takes a look at the wisdom of the world, which characterizes Jesus as nonsensical, even scandalous.

> *"But God chose the foolish things of the world to shame the wise; God chose the weak things of the world to shame the strong. God chose the lowly things of this world and the despised things—and the things that are not—to nullify the things that are" (1 Corinthians 1:27–28).*

Just spend a day on any college campus, and you'll find that God's Word is considered foolhardy, God's strength confused as weakness.

Simply looking foolish is enough for the world to push you aside. But that façade is really a gateway for God to start working in you because you're in it for the right reasons.

Living a Life of Yes means sometimes you'll look foolish. There's no guarantee that taking giant leaps of faith will make any sense at all.

I am trying to take to heart this suggestion from Puritan

author Jeremiah Burroughs: "If you hear others report this or that ill of you, and your hearts are dejected because you think you suffer in your name, your hearts were inordinately set on your name and reputation."[6]

If you have rarely said "yes," is it because you have never taken a risk, never gone off script, because you don't want to walk to a different beat than everyone else?

Love Bible promises? How about this one:

> *"If you were of the world, the world would love you as its own; but because you are not of the world, but I chose you out of the world, therefore the world hates you"* (John 15:19 ESV).

Other Bible verses promise you'll be chastised, ostracized, removed from society. You'll be an outsider, a nobody, a misfit, a lackey. You'll be the last one picked, the first one thrown out. You'll be mocked. Your words will fall on deaf ears. This is the way of the cross. There is no other way.

We need to embrace our "foolishness" because that is what will confound the "wise in their own eyes" (Proverbs 26:12). Don't flinch. Don't waver.

What Do You Dread the Most?

What if the life you've wanted, the future that you have dreamed of, is wrapped up in your worst fear?

Foolishness sometimes means losing everything. You may lose your identity. You may lose your good name. You will look like you have lost your mind.

We should be more afraid of missed opportunity than what things might go wrong.

I had a man I respected tell me as a youth that 95 percent of the things we worry about never come about. I haven't done the math, but after a lifetime of living, I can pretty much agree. Our fears are often unfounded.

A few years ago, I went up into my attic to replace a light fixture. It was stifling, cramped, and dark. I was afraid I was going to step through the ceiling, and the fiberglass itch set in almost immediately. I began to feel claustrophobic, which up to that point I had never experienced. All I know is that I needed to get out RIGHT NOW.

Did I conquer my fear?

No, I paid someone a hundred dollars to go up and change the bulb for me.

The Bible is replete with expressions of "Fear not." It shows up through the toughest of times: when warriors went into battle, when mortal men and women faced angels, and when ordinary folks felt like giving up.

No matter the odds, fear is something that should be given to God because He promises that He's got things under control. No matter how terrible things look, He promises that He's got our back—and He goes before us.

I was robbed at knifepoint once in Panama. It happened so quickly that I didn't have time to fear. I just handed over my wallet. But after the event, that's when the emotion and the dread hit my heart. Even though the robbery happened in broad daylight, for many years after I was looking over my shoulder.

So "fear not" for me was looking toward what happened before. I couldn't let my experience keep me from pressing on.

Philippians 3:13–14 says,

> *"Brothers and sisters, I do not consider myself yet to have taken hold of it. But one thing I do: Forgetting what is behind and straining toward what is ahead, I press on toward the goal to win the prize for which God has called me heavenward in Christ Jesus."*

What Would You Do If Fear Were Gone?

Of course, I was afraid when I stepped off the airplane in Jordan during the height of ISIS persecution.

I had no team. No posse. No backup plans.

"I am a Western journalist just dropping by to write about life in your county. Hey, are there any Christians around here?"

But by putting fear in its place, I was able to find—and to tell—God's story.

You don't have to go to a war zone, but you do have to go to war with the fear that holds you back. This lockstep with Jesus might lead to rejection in this world. Saying "yes" doesn't always mean you'll be accepted.

Maintaining the Christian life isn't a math equation. It's not a formula. It's not a three-step plan. It's a mystery. This whole walk is meant to be a mystery.

The disciples spent their entire time following Jesus, wondering and asking him what he was up to. Look at the questions. They were in a state of confusion. They didn't know what he was up to or why he was doing and saying what he was. And when he would explain why, they still didn't get it.

Embrace the discomfort.

Embrace the mystery.

Embrace your weakness.

Embrace the fear.

I only got those opportunities to make a difference when I forgot my credentials and leaned back and began to let God move.

That's a dangerous, but outrageously rewarding, way to live.

7

DON'T PLAY IT SAFE

"A ship in harbor is safe, but that is not what ships are built for."
—John Shedd

I constantly feel the tug to contain my joy, curb my fervor, and allow a little skepticism to tame my faith.

We're told that taking risks, embarking on foolish endeavors, and chasing dreams aren't the stuff of mature men and women. An act of maturity is to "settle down" with a path in life—and stick to it.

But the problem is that Easy Street is also a dead-end street. We have forgotten the thrills—and rewards—of danger. As if a protective parent were shouting in our heads, we hear the warnings.

We don't walk near the ledge because we might fall. But meanwhile, we miss a spectacular view.

We don't run down the mountain, hair flying in the wind, because we might trip. We miss the thrill of letting ourselves go.

We quit riding the merry-go-round because now it's suddenly scary. We neglect laughing so hard that our insides are turned out and our faces hurt with joy.

We don't love—and don't even try—because we have been hurt and we don't want to get hurt again.

Mike Yaconelli wrote a fabulous book called *Dangerous Wonder: The Adventure of Childlike Faith*. He says this: "I want a lifetime of holy moments. Every day I want to be in dangerous proximity to Jesus. I long for a life that explodes with meaning and is filled with adventure, wonder, risk, and danger. I long for a faith that is gloriously treacherous. I want to be with Jesus, not knowing whether to cry or laugh."[1]

Who played it safe in the Bible? The boy shepherd David? Abraham? Noah? Jacob? Mary? Peter? Paul? None of them.

Throughout the book of Acts, men and women were inspired, impassioned, emboldened. They kept saying "yes" and they changed the world.

How much space do you give to things you've never done before? Play the role of the novice, the rookie.

Do One Thing That Scares You

When I started my interest in and travels to the Middle East, I was an unlikely pilgrim. I had some background as a writer, with articles about leadership and management, even ghostwriting two successful books. But being a ghostwriter means you remain "unknown."

The Middle East. In a time of war. In a time of crisis. Who was I to go there? What could I offer to the region?

LIVING A LIFE OF YES

I had taught Sunday school to middle schoolers. I was just a middle-class Christian living in middle America experiencing my midlife. I wasn't even close to being prepared for the Middle East.

Ministering to Muslims? Writing about ISIS and the persecuted church? For me, these things were beyond any of my interests, but God was unleashed in my life, and I could feel His impact.

Let God surprise you. Testing God's creativity gives Him a great chance to rub His hands together and unleash a whole torrent of unexpected blessings.

Author Mary Schmich said, "Do one thing every day that scares you."

I believe everyone has a risk muscle. If you don't use it every day, it begins to atrophy, and soon you'll be too weak and tried to do something new.

Stepping Into the Role

My granddaughter Adalee loves the role of the princess. It's the result of too many Disney videos, sugar-crisp princess snacks, bedtime stories about castles, and endless marketing to the little girls of this world. Just about every adolescent girl thinks she has royal blood.

When she goes to her closet to pick out her clothes, she will always pick the fluffy princess skirts, ruffles, and lace.

One day she was dressed for the day in her imperial dress when she walked into my wife's secret shoe closet, the same one where dozens of shoes wait, hoping that this is the day they will come out of hiding. The shoe vault is in another bedroom of course, below the canopy of coats that are waiting their turn as well.

Adalee opened the door to this treasure chest. It wasn't long before she came walking out in my wife's two-inch heels—the ones that haven't been worn since the last wedding we attended. She giggled and then gave her royal wave, acting as if the shoes that were three times as big as her feet were perfectly normal. After all, she's a princess.

She has no idea of who or what she will be. At her tender age, she can stay simple. As she grows, she'll no doubt leave her princess stage, but I hope she'll never be afraid to step into shoes that don't fit.

I think there's something to be said for growing into your dreams.

Be Bold

When I was twenty-eight years old, I was a newly appointed postmaster in a little town outside Jackson Hole, Wyoming. I wore a tie to work. I swept the sidewalk and made sure all the forms were straight. I ran this office like it was my own little business. I could have stayed there forever.

Right away I joined the League of Postmasters, a fraternal order comprised of thirty thousand other leaders in post offices across the nation. Some were big, significant operations in large metro areas. Other postmasters led little offices like mine.

We had a state convention of postmasters right in my backyard, in Jackson, Wyoming. And why not? Jackson was perfect for any gathering.

I was eager to go and meet my peers, fellow postmasters from around the state. And we were even going to receive the national president of the organization, who was drawn to the natural beauty of the Tetons.

The proceedings started with the patriotic: the pledge of allegiance and a girls' choir singing the national anthem. The state president looked at the printed program, which called for morning prayer led by the state chaplain.

"Larry's car broke down in the canyon. He'll be here later," the master of ceremonies said. Larry Wisenbaker was the state chaplain, the honorary role given to a volunteer who helped bring a little God into the event.

"Since he's not here, we'll just move on," he said.

But then something moved inside me.

"I'll lead the prayer," I said. "I can do it."

I felt like Eddie Haskell in *Leave It to Beaver*. I was just a little too eager and a little too willing, but my boldness overcame any discomfort I felt. No one even really knew who I was, but who was going to say "no" to me?

I prayed out loud—and I wasn't meek about it. I prayed for the proceedings. I prayed for the community we were in. I prayed for the country that we all served. I prayed for our leadership, our nation, and the world. Six billion people later, I said "amen," which was followed by a surprising chorus of others who agreed with me.

The national president approached me later in the day, exchanging some pleasantries, welcoming me to the role of postmaster. He then talked about my boldness to pray.

"Where does that come from?" he asked.

I just smiled and looked up.

I then told him about my observation about the book of Acts—and how I tried to emulate those first-century believers. Throughout those early accounts of the church, we are often told about amazing gifts coming from the first apostles. I told him that many times they simply began speaking boldly (see Acts 4:13).

After I got done with my mini Bible study, he acknowledged his own faith and asked me to pray for him. And then he made an offer. Would I serve as the national chaplain?

Not knowing what it entailed, I said, "Yes."

I can say those ten years serving in that unpaid, unofficial role were the most formative in my life. Every month I penned an article that went to thirty thousand fellow postmasters. I spoke at conventions around the country. I preached to thousands at national conferences. I spoke to congressmen and senators on behalf of my organization when moral issues were at odds with postal policy.

As a young man this role gave me an opportunity to write. *Reuters Religion* picked up one of my columns and syndicated it one Sunday. Someone read that column and invited me to speak on a radio show. Someone else heard that radio show and encouraged me to write for their publication. That publication led to a part-time staff position with the *High Calling* where I later acted as a community editor. Someone at *Lifeway Publications* read an article I wrote and brought me into a recurring role for one of their magazines. That relationship led me to collaborate on two leadership books by a leadership foundation in Alabama.

None of this would have happened if I hadn't said "yes" that first time. I jumped into a role I had no place taking on.

Be bold once—you'll never know where that will lead.

Unbuckle Your Seat Belt

I mentioned my stint at the *High Calling*. This was a beautiful community where we highlighted voices from around the country, focusing on vocation, art, and purpose. One year, staff members were invited to a retreat at Laity Lodge, near Leakey, Texas. This beautiful 1,900-acre ranch retreat center, founded and funded by the H. E. Butt Foundation, is a little piece of heaven. Camps for youth and families have filled Frio River Canyon with shouts of joy for decades. And the retreat center has hosted some of the greatest thinkers and artists this side of heaven for many years.

One of the most intriguing aspects of the property is the entry. After passing through miles and miles of large Texas ranches, the ranch road, a small two-lane highway, drops down into the valley through a dirt road. The road follows the river until the narrowing canyon squeezes out the pavement. And just like that, there is no more road, and the vehicle is driving on the river bed.

Just a few inches deep, the hard-rock river bed is perfect for vehicles. It was an exhilarating moment when we arrived at this point because I had never done anything like that in my life. We all leaned out our windows and ran our hands on the splashing water, wiping the drops from our faces.

But one woman who was riding with us didn't enjoy the moment. I motioned her to lean and touch the river at the sides of the vehicle. She couldn't bring herself to take off her seat belt because it was "the law." She missed the thrill.

I felt sorry for her. But she's not alone. Much of the world is obsessed with safety and predictability and rules. We have a structure that is imposed at every level—the government, the church, the workplace. Every rule or law that is imposed is a result of trial and error in human experimentation. Once planners find something that works for the good of society or the workplace, then they create a standard.

But we allow adherence to work its way into our lives so much that it doesn't let us live. We stick to playing it safe, to following these well-worn standards.

If you start *Living a Life of Yes*, you might have to break a few rules. And that rogue nature is going to create some challenges for those nearest you. Your friends will think you have lost your senses. Your family will sometimes throw up their hands. Your closest friends will wonder about you.

It goes with the territory. But then He shows up and keeps nudging you back.

When Jesus Showed Up at the Diner

Early on in this book project, my wife and I spent one day mapping out ideas. We had flip chart sheets full of ideas all over the living room. My stream of consciousness was flowing, and she was rapidly trying to keep up. But like a dog with a short attention span, my ideas were all over the place.

At the end of the day we were both spent; we hoped we had made some progress, but the disorganization left us uncertain.

We went out to the Denver Diner, a brightly lit institution that never closes in the heart of the city. The big plates of hash browns and eggs are just the right comfort food for hungry students as well as the homeless nursing a cup of coffee against the evening cold.

We went just for the pie. We ordered one lemon meringue, one chocolate silk. "No, we're not sharing," my wife told me.

I got up to use the restroom, and a younger man sitting with another couple in a booth on the far side of the restaurant looked me straight into my eyes as I passed him. He said, "Are you working on that book?" He looked at the other two, and they all burst into muffled laughter.

I went into the bathroom and looked at myself in the mirror. *How did they know that?* I was immediately self-conscious. Still, the detail of the question was eerily accurate.

I returned to my seat, but within a couple minutes I couldn't sit. I got up and knelt next to their table.

"Why did you ask that question?" I said to the young man.

He said, "I don't know. It just came to me."

His companion said, "God talks to him a lot." The woman nodded her head. "Yes. He does."

I then confessed that, yes, I had been working on a book all day and had come to the diner to get a little break because it just wasn't feeling right.

The other man said, "I think God is telling you to write that book." The woman spoke up and said, "It is a Christian book, right?"

Shaking my head, I was too stunned by the insight from these three. They asked me if I was going to church the next day. I said, "Yes. It's not far from here."

One by one they challenged each other to go. "We really need this," the first young man said. "We all do," said the woman.

I went back to my pie, not even sure of what to say to my wife.

"I think I just met Jesus. Even He is saying 'yes.'"

Reject a Life of Mediocrity

I brought the report card home for the required parental signature and coolly dropped it in my mom's purse, hoping she would just sign it off.

No such luck. In our home, this was a significant event. She saw the C in social studies and for the next hour, it seemed, talked to me about what "average" meant. There would be no average in our family. We came from a proud line of immigrants who fought and struggled to survive. The men in the family were sailors and farmers and gas station owners. None of them were rich, but none of them were average. I had heard the story a hundred times before.

The next day, my mom went down to the school, without an appointment, to visit the teacher. I cringed inside. And of course the truth came out that day. I had been slacking, more concerned with being a kid than being a scholar.

"You can do better" was the message from the teacher. "If only you would apply yourself."

While perfectionism is worldly and frustrating, excellence is God ordained. But there's another danger in looking for a happy medium: mediocrity, which takes from the worst of both worlds.

We think grace lets us off the hook because there's no scorecard. Paul exhorts us not to use our freedom as "an opportunity for the flesh" (Galatians 5:13 ESV). And my flesh is mediocrity. I settle. I get soft. I lean heavy on that crutch and miss my chance to change the world.

I think that's the difference. Perfectionism sucks the life out of a person. Mastery honors God by using the gifts He has imparted to us.

Mediocrity is a black hole so powerful that great ideas and innovation are drawn in, never to come back out.

Mediocrity takes all the brights that color our world and absorbs them into empty pixels.

And living in a mediocre world isn't much fun. It would be void of creativity, innovation, and adventure. How terrible if everyone just played it safe? In fact, it would be plain boring.

God doesn't care much for mediocrity either. The lukewarm church of Laodicea was addressed by name in the book of Revelation (Revelation 3:14–22). The message to Laodicea was one of judgment with a call to repentance. "I know your deeds, that you are neither cold nor hot. I wish you were either one or the other! So, because you are lukewarm—neither hot nor cold—I am about to spit you out of my mouth" (Revelation 3:15–16).

I've been to Laodicea, which is found in modern-day Turkey. The archaeology shows their water supply likely came from an aqueduct sourced at a hot mineral springs five miles away. By the time the water worked its way to the city, it was tepid. If you were drinking this water, you wouldn't keep it in your mouth.

To me, the message in Revelation shouts against mediocrity. Stand up! Stand tall! Stand for what you've been given!

Acting small doesn't do a thing for the world. Minimizing your talents wastes the investments that others and God have placed in you. Playing it safe doesn't impact your workplace, your school, or your family. When you say, "I'm nothing special," you're questioning not only your God-given talents but also the belief others have in you and the trust of those you influence.

You can sit back and play dormant like everyone else, but it's killing you on the inside.

You don't bring pleasure to God by trying to be someone else.

> "You have no right to argue with your Creator. You are merely a clay pot shaped by a potter. The clay doesn't ask, 'Why did you make me this way?'" (Isaiah 45:9 CEV).

Not Everyone Is Convinced to Leap

I realize writing a book like this can alienate some readers. This talk about diving into the pool, leaping into the future, and launching into space might make you uncomfortable.

Our culture is obsessed with safety, isn't it? Last week I read a state-mandated warning at the coffee shop about the hazards of caffeine. We routinely tear off long tags on strollers about all the ways your baby can get injured. Read the fine print on your prescription medicine—you're a goner.

If you are a mother, you don't use bottles with BPA. You have locked your kitchen cabinets. You have put bumpers on the edges of your tables. Give a child to a mother, and instantly that child is enveloped in safety. The whole world knows, "No one will harm this child."

My wife is not always a willing participant in all these schemes. She came from a broken home and a broken marriage and spent most of her adult life as a single mom. Security, safety, and protection are part of her DNA.

When the road before us diverges, and the choices are "paved" or "dirt," I'm wheeling onto the dirt road. Meanwhile, she's often advocating for the paved. She's the voice of reason, and she's kept me from killing myself or at least doing something stupid or destructive.

But she's been stretching and learning. Along this journey, she's met new people and been introduced to new situations. She's experiencing this life of "yes" and reaping the benefits.

I believe every person wants to lead a life of significance. In this world of Instagram superstars and Pinterest heroes, maybe you won't necessarily travel the world promoting peace, but you can impact your neighbor with love. You don't have to bring about a great revival, but you can work on reconciliation in your family. You likely won't get the chance to have thousands hang on your every word, but you can speak truth into a difficult community situation.

Every one of those requires you to say "yes."

Every one of those will challenge your security.

Who promised that life would be orderly, unchallenged, and without discomfort? No one. The construct we have built is that life should be safe, and I'm here to poke a hole in that theory.

Not ready to dive all the way in? You have kids. You have a spouse. You have your own future. I get it. Would you consider the 14-Day *Living a Life of Yes* Challenge at the end of this book? Just try saying "yes" for two weeks and see where you will land.

8

GET READY TO CHANGE THE WORLD

"How wonderful it is that nobody need wait a single moment before starting to improve the world."
—Anne Frank

Let me tell you a short story about a man named Milt.

He was a pastor by trade, but he spent his early morning hours watching warblers, spotting starlings, and tracking terns.

He had a fascination with birds. He studied them with intense attraction. He built a massive library on the subject, and his two sons thought him a little . . . off. But like most kids, they kind of let the old man do his thing.

In the summer of 1889, Milt's twenty-five-year-old son Orville contracted a fever. It turned into delirium, and he almost died. He would recover, but it would take many long weeks to restore his health.

Orville's brother, Will, sat with him through the recovery, even after moving from the hospital back home. To pass the time, the two settled into their father's expansive study with the big windows.

They began pulling those bird books off the shelves and settled on one in particular—*Animal Mechanism: A Treatise on Terrestial and Aerial Locomotion.*

It was a book about the body, bone, and feather structure of birds and how they are outfitted for flight. They took the book another step—beyond birds. They began to dream about what it would take for a man to fly.

After his recovery, Orville began to nudge his brother into taking their dreams to flight. The man who almost died of fever began to soar in his thinking.

He even wrote the Smithsonian asking for their help, as Mark Batterson summarizes in his book *In a Pit with a Lion on a Snowy Day*, to "convince the world to repent of its lack of belief in flight."[1]

It was Bishop Milton Wright's interest in birds that turned into a passion. That passion sparked his sons' dreams and obsession. The Wright brothers changed the world forever with their flying machines.

You might not launch men into flight.

You might not be the one with your heads in the clouds.

But your keen interest might just help inspire someone else.

You never know your circle of influence. You might just change the world by simply being you!

LIVING A LIFE OF YES

What's That in Your Hand?

Do you feel like you are just not cut out to carry the load you've been burdened with? Feel like you're too old, not smart enough, too young, not experienced enough. Name the excuse—we can all relate.

Responsibility has a way of sneaking up on us. Suddenly the project at work is yours. Or the small group looks to you to lead. All eyes are on you, and everyone is expecting you to take charge.

I remember bringing our son, James, home from the hospital. The survival of this baby was entirely up to a twenty-year-old mother and a twenty-two-year-old father.

We were responsible not just to change his diapers, but to feed him, to keep him away from danger, and to keep him alive.

What was God thinking? I was in no shape to have that responsibility. Somehow, James survived because I had the hidden tools to be a father.

It's one thing to be responsible for a family; it's entirely another thing to be responsible for an entire nation, indeed an entire lineage.

That's what Moses felt. The burden of responsibility heavy on his shoulders. The Egyptian sun beating down on his shoulders and the voice of God echoing in his mind.

Remember the burning bush? Moses was tending the flock of his father-in-law when God spoke out of the burning bush. God went on and described the misery of the people, how they were oppressed and how they needed to be rescued. I can see Moses nodding his head. Yes, yes, YES!

Then God dropped the bomb: "So now, go. I am sending

you to Pharaoh to bring my people the Israelites out of Egypt" (Exodus 3:10).

Moses answered just like I would. "Who am I that I should go to Pharaoh and bring the Israelites out of Egypt?" (Exodus 3:11).

Well, God gave him a sign of empowerment. And it was something Moses was already carrying in his hand. A staff—a big walking stick.

Normally it was just a piece of wood, but then God would turn it into a snake, or a weapon, or a divider of the waters. It looked like a stick, but it represented power. Just when Moses needed it the most.

So, you ask, "Who am I to do this big thing? Who am I to say 'yes,' to dive into responsibility for others, to carry truth and administer righteousness? Who am I to write this, to speak this, to do this?"

And God says, "Grab that stick and let's go for a walk."

Here's the math. Whoever You Already Are + God's Amazing Power = What You Need.

Now that you have a little stick, it's time to get a little swagger.

Jump-start Your Enthusiasm

There is a saying, "Set yourself on fire with enthusiasm and people will come for miles to watch you burn."

It sounds shocking—but it's true.

There is something about enthusiasm that is contagious. Just think about your own life. You want to be around people who are moving forward, who have a vision and can rally people.

I want you to become that person, someone so inspiring that others will follow. To be this kind of person, you need three things:

- **Purpose** for what you do
- **Passion** for the vision
- **Persistence** in the action

Let's start with **purpose**.

Several men were carrying bricks outside a construction site in the 1600s in Renaissance Italy. A curious bystander asked the sweating men what they were doing.

One man said, "I am moving rocks."

Another man said, "I am helping build a wall."

A third man said, "I am building a cathedral to the Almighty."

Which one went home with more enthusiasm? Which one rallied the troops, helped increase donations, and led an army?

Purposeful living will help find a reason to get out of bed every day. It will help you push through the uncomfortable. It will help you take one more step into the unknown.

Another mark of enthusiasm is **passion.**

Where do people get passion from? Have you ever been part of something so exciting, you just had to join in? Maybe it was a softball team that was winning, or a work group that was full of ideas, or a neighborhood cleanup project.

Passion is infectious. Enthusiasm is unstoppable. That is until someone throws a wet blanket on it all. Have you ever had a great idea only to have your wings clipped, your legs cut out below you?

A cynic is someone who, when he smells flowers, looks around for a coffin. Toxic people find ways to ruin your day.

Ignore them.

Passion starts with you. Somebody's watching you, and they are looking to you for signs.

Antoine de Saint-Exupéry, the storied French aristocrat who volunteered to fly reconsonisance missions into Nazi territory, said, "If you want to build a ship, don't drum up your men to go to the forest to gather wood, saw it, and nail the planks together. Instead, teach them the desire for the sea."

A few years ago, I spent a summer evening in Cleveland, and while I was there, I took in an Indians baseball game at Progressive Field. As I entered through the gates, excitement gripped me. Thirty thousand fans all stuffed into the new baseball park with the green grass and smells of popcorn was enough to make my spine tingle.

As the game began, it was quickly apparent to the disappointed crowd that the home team was about to be blown out. The ace pitcher for the visiting Angels smothered the Indians' bats. Conversely, the Angels' hitters were battering the ball with a torrid combination of base hits. The score was 9–0 in the third inning. Essentially, the game was over. The home crowd was growing restless. Every Angels run was greeted with stoic silence, broken only by the cleats of the batter as he crossed the plate.

Then I saw a commotion in the seats in the next deck below me. One person would stand up, raise her arms, arch her back, and shout. Soon the person next to her did it. Then the number grew to about fifteen. Soon the entire section caught the frenzy. It wasn't long before the stadium was participating in one of modern sports' most treasured inventions: The Wave. It circled the stadium time and again with the participants never tiring. It was thrilling to see it in action. The Indians, however, were in their dugout, perhaps feeling the pain of their failure to entertain their own fans.

I was impressed that a stadium full of fans could be so enthused about The Wave when the primary purpose of their trip to the park was now gone. They were oblivious to the failure of their heroes.

You might feel like you are all alone. You may be sad and blue. The home team may be a miserable failure. Wherever you may be, whatever your situation, stand up. Stand up and cheer. Soon you will be joined by two or three others. With some perseverance, you can affect an entire town.

We can do The Wave across America, in our churches, in our neighborhoods, in our families.

Maybe, just possibly, we can affect an entire culture.

And the final step is **persistence.**

Agostino di Duccio, an Italian sculptor, worked on a piece of marble that was difficult to sculpt. Eventually he gave up, claiming he could not do anything with it. He let go of the dream of the masterpiece he had envisioned.

Other sculptors inherited the wieldy piece of marble, and one by one, each gave up. It was too difficult to work with.

The marble came into the possession of Michelangelo. He envisioned the timeless possibilities in the stubborn stone. His final work was unveiled as the timeless sculpture *David.*

The message is clear. Don't give up. You may have those rough pieces of rock in your workplace, home, or circle of friends. With enough patience, persistence, and hard work, there just might be a masterpiece waiting.

You must keep at it. You can't give up. You must be creative. There is a solution, and it's your job to find it.

Enthusiasm comes naturally for some people. You know them by name. They can weather any storm, endure any insult, smile through any situation. They infect everyone around them with their boundless zeal.

Henry Ford, the automobile manufacturer, had this to say about enthusiasm: "You can do anything if you have enthusiasm. Enthusiasm is the sparkle in your eye, it is the swing in your gait, the grip of your hand, the irresistible surge of your will and your energy to execute your ideas. Enthusiasm is at the bottom of all progress. With it, there is an accomplishment. Without it, there are only alibis."

Float a Line of Hope

The Niagara Falls suspension bridge was an idea born in the fertile mind of William Merritt in 1846.

Most experts agreed: it couldn't be done. The span was too high, and nobody had overcome this engineering feat.

But Merritt wouldn't give up. While watching children fly their kites over the falls, an idea took form. He sponsored a contest and paid five dollars to the first one who could loft their kite to the other side, where it was captured and secured with a strong stake.

Meticulously, he strung a larger cord across the divide, using the kite string as a guide. Then he pulled across a heavier line, then a rope and finally a wire cable which was the beginning of this new bridge.

Building a better world sometimes means working against impossible odds. Critics on both sides of the water will tell you it cannot be done. But if you can float a string of hope across the chasm, it may one day lead to a permanent bridge for all.

Don't Wait for Doors to Open by Themselves

We often wait around waiting for God to open doors.

While "I'm waiting for Him to show me what to do next" sounds spiritual, it really limits your opportunities to experience what He has in store for you.

The whole faith experience isn't just stepping forward at the start and saying, "I trust." When you commit to God, you sign up for a lifetime of uncertainty, doubt, and wavering. Only by opening doors do you see what's on the other side. And then you gain perfect clarity.

Sometimes you open one door only to see another. That's what happened to me when I started in this venture. One door didn't necessarily lead to another room, but it did lead to other opportunities.

Author Deidra Riggs once wrote on her blog about a *Sesame Street* cartoon sketch that featured a little boy and a girl who found their plant had wilted overnight.

Using their childlike reasoning, they found different ways to revive the drooping plant, thinking it was simply asleep. They talked to it in progressively louder voices. They invited the dog to come in and bark. They used an alarm clock. They used a sliding trombone.

Finally, they poured a glass of water into the soil, and the plant slowly lifted to life.

That kind of trial and error doesn't show a lack of faith. It helps us define the problem, work on solutions, and define answers. By working through the issues, you'll find what works and what doesn't. That's what we call "progress." The trombone wasn't a failure. It was a solution that wasn't appropriate for the problem.

Deidra summed it up like this: "When a door opens up for you, step through it. You don't need to overthink it and try to figure out what will happen next if you step through the door. All you need to do is to step through that door and that door alone. Then, wait to see which door opens next and, when it does, step through that one."[2]

Expect to Be Surprised

I wish I could promise health, wealth, and prosperity in your life. While these blessings might come your way, I'm not certain it's going to roll out like that.

But you will be surprised, and delighted—regularly.

We have a dear friend who gives and gives and gives. Every single day of her life is dedicated to others. With just a few pennies to her name, she'll give up every single one of them to someone in need. She gives away so much that her friends and family get mad at her.

But that doesn't deter her.

It was bad news when we found out her car was on its last leg, no doubt from scrambling across the city with groceries or picking up women released from prison or shuttling the elderly to doctor appointments.

"What are you going to do?" I offered to help with my minor mechanic abilities, but the problems were above my skill level. She just shrugged her shoulders. "God will provide." But her circle of friends and those she had helped throughout the years started scrambling, raising money for another car.

In the first day, thousands had poured in. That evening, I was in a conversation with my next-door neighbor who was helping an elderly friend clear out her estate. He told me how the estate had an extra, low-mileage vehicle. "How should I advertise it?" he asked. I told him not to bother.

Of course, when we presented the keys and the car to our friend, she was reluctant. After all, she was the giver. But part of saying "yes" means saying "yes" to others who provide for you. "Let others bless you," I said to her. When others get to participate, the blessing doubles.

All her days she had said "yes" to poverty. She said "yes" to uncertainty. In return, her needs were met abundantly.

Letting Go—Why Is It So Hard?

During one of my Jordan excursions, I visited the shores of the Dead Sea. At more than 1,400 feet below sea level, it's the lowest spot on earth.

A friend I was with collected some of the mud from the shore and smeared it on himself. The $200 mud treatments charged by spas around the world can be had with a scoop of the hand here. It seemed silly to do this—and challenged my predetermined sense of manliness—but I followed suit. I let it bake on while facing the burning sun, and I could feel the salt lifting the oils from my skin. Don't count on any future updates from me on facial mud masks!

But the real experience was to float in the waters of the Dead Sea. With a 34 percent salinity, it's one of the world's saltiest bodies of water. It's nine times saltier than the ocean. Nothing lives in these waters—no fish, no plant life. Not even bacteria.

The Jordan River continually dumps fresh, vibrant water

into the Dead Sea. But after that, every living thing is choked out by the salt. The sea has one inlet and no outlets. There are relationships like this, and homes, and churches. There are people who take and never give. There is no lower place a human can sink . . . no lower place on earth for them to reside.

I entered the waters with my muddy body, and before I could even begin to ease into the water, my feet began to rise. Like a gravity effect, my body began to float. I tried a few strokes from my side and on my back, but the traditional trajectory and movements of my body were thwarted by the water which pushed harder against my efforts.

I tried turning to my front, but the water flipped me over like a bathtub toy. The ballast was on my front side. I was a human cork, bobbing, floating. I yelled to my pal across the water, "Help me, I can't drown!"

And it was true. It is impossible to die of drowning in these waters.

I tried the different strokes taught to me by Mrs. Jacobs when I was nine. Sidestroke. Frog push. Forward stroke. Nothing worked. It was useless.

The only enjoyment I had was when I lay back in the water and let go. I released my efforts and lay prone on my back—and let go. I had to trust the water that I had grown to fear all my life.

Over one shoulder I could see the green rolling hills of Israel. On the other side I could see the Jordanian resorts. Straight up I could see the sky. I closed my eyes to the quiet and bobbed with the gentle waves, not a care in the world.

It took plenty of trust to believe that salt was going to keep me afloat in that water. But it did. It meant letting go of all that

I knew about water. It meant letting go of all the things I'd been told about nature and the supernatural.

I finally understood what it meant to let go that day in the Dead Sea. That day I could do nothing but float and believe. I spent the evening deep in thought. The sun set across the mysterious waters. My skin, refreshingly vibrant. My soul, ready for the next act of surrender.

9

SAYING "YES" ISN'T ALWAYS EASY

*"Have I not commanded you? Be strong and courageous. Do not be frightened, and do not be dismayed, for the L*ORD *your God is with you wherever you go." —Joshua 1:9 (ESV)*

Once you start *Living a Life of Yes*, fulfilling a dream, you'll meet difficulties. You have a vision, and you'll chase it. But along the way, rather than rallying others to the cause, you are met with questioning eyebrows, lifted high in disapproval. You don't get one shred of encouragement.

And then you hit a wall. Or a ditch. Or a cliff. Call it what you want, but the dream has a big problem.

So you sit back and evaluate. It doesn't make sense.

It's not supposed to!

One of the strange anomalies of the man who preached in the Middle East two thousand years ago is that he spoke in upside-down language.

- If you want to save your life, you must lose it.
- To be lifted up, you must humble yourself.
- To be the greatest, you must be the servant of all.
- To be the first, you must be the last.
- If you want to be in charge, you must serve.
- If you want to be strong, you must be weak.
- To inherit the riches of heaven, you must be poor in spirit.

Jesus lost a lot of people with this single Sermon on the Mount (Matthew 5:3–10). It just didn't make sense.

Living a Life of Yes might not ever line up logically. If you are waiting for all the answers to line up, for all this to make perfect sense, you'll wait your entire life and miss out on what you are supposed to be doing.

If you are waiting for the right time, the seconds and hours and days and weeks and years will start piling up until you are out of time.

If you are waiting until you have enough money, or enough support, or enough resources, you'll spend everything you have been given and, in the end, have nothing.

If you are waiting until all fear is gone, you'll never have enough confidence.

Moses was given a big vision by God. He stood on Mount Nebo, and God pointed to the boundaries that he had drawn for his new nation.

I stood on Mount Nebo, on the very spot that Moses pondered his future. I imagined my future, looking to the east and the west and the north and south. I could see the Jordan below and the land of Israel to my left and my right.

The wind rustled the dried leaves. I heard the distant barking of a dog. I wondered what it was like for Moses.

Moses never was able to take the land. He died on the wrong side of the Jordan, and he was buried by God on the very mountain where he first saw the promise.

It was Joshua who later took up the mantle of leadership. The vision was passed to him, and he was the one who would lead the people. He knew there were big grapes in the promised land. But he also knew there were big giants to face.

Joshua was given an equally big task by God to take the land.

It wasn't enough to name the promise. It wasn't enough to claim it as his own. He had to possess it.

"I will give you every place where you set your foot" was God's promise (Joshua 1:3).

It was going to be hard work. "Now then, you and all these people, get ready to cross the Jordan River into the land I am about to give to them" (Joshua 1:2).

In Joshua's case, nothing would come easy. There would be sweat and tears. There would be bloodshed.

So, although this land, this promise, was a gift, Joshua and the people were going to have to fight for it.

Sometimes we think gifts are things that we open, simply untying the bow and ripping off the paper. But those kinds of gifts don't always last.

The true gifts in life are the things we must fight for, the things that come with a struggle.

Make a list of the things in your life that mean something. For me, it's easy. God. Family. Career. Every one of those things came through sacrifice, struggle, and even pain.

The Struggle That Leads to Life

The promise came in Joshua 1, and we put the words on coffee mugs and in greeting cards. "Be strong and courageous. . . . for the LORD your God will be with you wherever you go" (Joshua 1:9).

God told Joshua that he needed strength and courage—as well as His presence. These weren't throwaway words. Because this fabled promised land wasn't the great frontier of the Middle East. It wasn't like a land grab where men on horses rode into the distance to claim their forty acres. These lands were occupied by kings and armies. They would be opposed to the bitter end.

> *"The lands included the hill country, the western foothills, the Arabah, the mountain slopes, the wilderness, and the Negev. These were the lands of the Hittites, Amorites, Canaanites, Perizzites, Hivites and Jebusites" (Joshua 12:8).*

In the preceding chapters, we are given blow-by-blow descriptions of great battles. And by the time we get to chapter 12, we are given a list of all the kings who had fallen (Joshua 12:9–25):

- The king of Jericho
- The king of Ai
- The king of Jerusalem
- The king of Hebron
- The king of Jarmuth
- The king of Lachish
- The king of Eglon

- The king of Gezer
- The king of Debir
- The king of Geder
- The king of Hormah
- The king of Arad
- The king of Libnah
- The king of Adullam
- The king of Makkedah
- The king of Bethel
- The king of Tappuah
- The king of Hepher
- The king of Aphek
- The king of Lasharon
- The king of Madon
- The king of Hazor
- The king of Shimron Meron
- The king of Akshaph
- The king of Taanach
- The king of Megiddo
- The king of Kedesh
- The king of Jokneam in Carmel
- The king of Dor
- The king of Goyim in Galgal
- The king of Tirzah

That's a total of thirty-one kings who fell. Behind every one of them were men of war, trained to defend their land.

If you want to be a part of a bigger story, it's going to cost you. And before you take on the promise, you must realize that you might have to give something up.

I had a dream to write this book. It was years in the making, and I resisted the promise because I knew it was going to cost me.

I love to fly-fish and to camp. I love festivals and gatherings and concerts. I love getting together with people from work and church. At first I wasn't willing to give that up for the sake of these words, but once I realized that the dream would not go away, I knew the sacrifice would be worth it.

With every land promised comes a battle of some sort. But in our nature we don't like conflict. And when we start down a path, too often we stop at the first sign of conflict.

We are mistaken when we think God's way is an easy way. We think the will of God is a straight highway. But it's not. It's full of potholes, construction zones, and detours.

Your destiny depends on your ability not only to walk but to fight. That's not a word we like. When it comes to your choice of fight or flight, most of us run. It's human nature to protect ourselves, our finances, our time, and our future.

Or maybe you don't fight to the end. You get a little taste of the promised land, and then you stop. "This is enough. There's no need to keep pressing on."

We get satisfied. We get content. We get lazy.

Maybe we're not patient enough. How long do we have to keep saying "yes"? One month? One year? I say it's a *lifetime* of saying "yes" because sometimes the fight takes that long.

What's the Worst Thing That Could Happen?

As we have been living this "yes" life, my wife has often been the voice of reason and protection. Her role is appreciated and keeps me from saying "yes" to the things that might just ruin us.

That reason also keeps things in perspective. As we evaluate options in different scenarios, she asks a great question: "What's the worst thing that could happen?"

If you aren't a person of faith, this question is relevant. Even the greatest of fears have minimal downside. It's a simple risk-ratio proposition. If you perform a specific action, then what is the risk? For example, more than 70 percent of people have a fear of flying. But the odds of dying as a plane passenger are one in 205,552. That compares with odds of one in 4,050 for dying as a cyclist, one in 1,086 for drowning, and one in 102 for dying in a car crash.

For the person of faith, we don't use statistics in the same way. We are told that the person who loses everything will gain everything, the last will be first, the servant will be the leader, and the foolish will be wise. In God's upside-down world, maybe we will lose everything. But we are promised we'll get it all back again.

Jesus said in Mark 8:35 (TLB), "If you insist on saving your life, you will lose it. Only those who throw away their lives for my sake and for the sake of the Good News will ever know what it means to really live." I will gladly fall flat in this world if I'm upright in the next.

I heard about a pastor with Impact Ministries in India. He was a convert from Hinduism and went back to his village to minister to his friends and family.

He was greeted with taunts and threats. They eventually made good on those threats. They burned his belongings right down to his clothing. They didn't stop there. They burned his home. That forced him out to the woods to live. Still, he came back to town to help his townspeople with basic needs and to speak the truth.

His love eventually won many of them over to Christ. And

within a few months, the same people who burned his house, now with a new set of priorities, built a new home for this man.

That's losing . . . and living.

Don't Be a Stranger to Danger

It looked terrible as he clutched his wrist and grimaced in pain. Joshua was just eleven, and he was all boy. He had been stunt jumping on his bicycle and had "biffed it," adolescent talk for "had a major accident and lived to tell."

That was my son. And he gives great grief—and joy.

The wrist was broken. This was the third broken bone in three successive summers. The poor kid thought that summer vacation in a cast was normal. He didn't whine. He didn't mope. It was a two-hour diversion from the rest of summer. He played baseball, football, and soccer with that cast. We went to the Gulf of Mexico, and we outfitted him with a waterproof sleeve that was bright blue, warning the underwater world that this was a boy not to be messed with.

Throughout the rest of the year, he was usually sporting bandages, wraps, compresses, or casts. Any day, I expected some overly sensitive child protective services agent to knock on the door, waving papers. I was ready to fight for my son's right to be a boy.

Joshua is known for his persistent smile and engaging personality. But that vivacious spirit also took him down many run-ins with teachers in school, as they didn't always appreciate his joyful demeanor.

Part of being a wild child also meant he took risks. He wrecked cars and snowmobiles and bikes. We spent more time in emergency rooms than I care to remember. Stitches, bandages, and antiseptic were second nature. One time in high school, he was working at a smoothie bar, and rather than scoop ice cream in a normal fashion, he pulled out the scoop like an Old West fighter, six-gun drawn. But on the spin of the weapon, the scoop cut his finger to the bone. And he later ended up with a bone infection that meant infusions. Nothing was ever easy with Josh, but he has always been the most amazing human being—fun, loyal, and engaging.

All those medical experiences triggered something in him, as he now is a top-notch emergency room nurse, working in a trauma center. I can imagine him visiting with patients as they come in. I wonder how many little boys he's cared for over the years, and I bet he looks at them with a knowing look. "Dude, I did that too."

There is something about living on the edge that is dismissed as foolishness in our grown-up society. People are taking all the fun out of being a kid. There's a new report about how dangerous bouncy castles are! Really? "Ban them," they cry.

Josh wore his casts with pride, happily retelling the exploits behind them. I thought they would ruin his summers, but they were testaments to a life lived well. And to this date, he has a list of scars and a story behind every one of them.

Living dangerously sounds scary. But once you've ducked under the "Do Not Cross" tape, you're one step closer to joy.

My problem is that I have mistaken dangerous things for stupid things and made tragic mistakes that were just plain dumb. I've spent a lifetime sorting out the difference.

And there is a call to exercise my faith dangerously. It means following that nudge to do the right thing, even when public opinion is against me. It means walking the high wire to reach the other side where the untouchables, the broken, are. It means living on the edge of popular culture with a distinctively unpopular message.

But there's a fine line between being bold and being unwise.

There's No Need to Be Stupid

Saying "yes" doesn't mean you have a license to be foolhardy.

Jumping off big cliffs with no safety rope is close to having a death wish. Taking chances on unreliable people can be a recipe for failure. Not having money or education or a groundswell of support is risky.

There is a difference between having faith and being just plain dumb.

I've been to the Middle East without support. I thought I made wise choices. Many people thought me foolish. I had a family and friends back home who were praying for me and counting on me to return. I had a future in front of me.

There is a difference between "faith" and "foolishness." Don't substitute the two, and don't use this book as an excuse to put yourself or your family in danger.

That's not what we're talking about here. And if you're not sure, take a step back. Breathe, speak with others, and pray until you can discern the difference.

But if you press forward, it will likely come at a cost.

It Might Cost You

I recently met a man who had an incredible story to tell. I'll call this cop James because what he did could lead to severe ramifications for his career and pension.

With more than four decades in law enforcement, he had

seen it all—the guilty and the victims, the oppressor and the oppressed. Dealing with everything from street thugs to white-collar crime, he always fought the deep dive into cynicism. He did so with a mix of humor and strength.

This was a man who filled just about every police role possible. He had been a street cop, SWAT team member, and police lieutenant. He had supervisory roles and had seen it all.

He spent his final fifteen years as a bailiff. And this is where he found his calling, looking to make a difference.

At nearly six and a half feet tall, the big man with broad shoulders and deep voice is not to be messed with physically. If you want a fight, he can bring it.

As a bailiff, James's duties included moving prisoners in and out of their holding areas on their way to and from the court. He knew he only had a minute with every prisoner, and he looked to make it count.

He tells the story about one prisoner, whom we are calling William. By chance—or divine appointment—James was on his way out of the courtroom when his eyes caught William's; there was a connection he couldn't shake. It wasn't the anger or the frustration that he usually saw from the accused. It was pain . . . and sadness.

William was in his cell, waiting for his court appearance. He would be pleading for a fifteen-year sentence. He asked James about the process, where he would be going after the plea went through.

And James simply spoke truth into the prisoner's life.

"You need a change of heart, not a change of location," he said. "When you get to prison, find Jesus. Find others who are talking about Jesus. There, you can find true change."

For four months he prayed for William and finally started to dig. He found out the prison he had been sent to. With much hesitation, he penned a letter. "You don't know me, but I saw you earlier this year in court."

They began exchanging letters, and four months later my friend suddenly realized that he could be disciplined or even fired for the breach in protocol.

"I had to do it. God was very clear," he said.

He still said "yes," choosing to follow the lead of God in his life and trusting Him for the results.

The first letter led to a return letter and then multiple correspondences. After a year and a half of prayer, encouragement, and open discussion, William gave his life to God.

Today, William is a free man, and he and James are close friends. It's an odd relationship. An older white man with a lifetime steeped in law enforcement breaking bread with a thirty-something black man who has a life of trouble behind him.

But it's the story of a changed life. William is in college, sporting straight As. He's been working to establish connections with his children.

James's wife was particularly challenged by this relationship.

"I knew nothing of this side of life and chose to isolate myself from my husband's work. I tend to be fearful and easily intimated. But together we jumped with William."

She calls the change in all of them "amazing."

"We love him dearly."

This story perfectly illustrates saying "yes" despite the consequences.

My friend and his wife are now working as mentors and friends to William. His wife told me that they "call him a son."

"And all I ever knew about the hood was how to spell it," she said to me. "I couldn't believe my husband took that step, but we answered the call of God."

Sure, my friend could have been fired, but then he would have spent the rest of his life wondering what he might have missed.

The Ultimate Sacrifice

Doing the daring thing might mean you lose out on a job, or a promotion, or status. It might even cost you your life.

I've met amazing people on this journey, many with happy stories. But there is a different trajectory for a woman I met named Semse Aydin. She has endured the hardest of all burdens, and yet she wouldn't live any other way except to say "yes."

I interviewed her in the living room of a friend and was impressed by her humble resilience.

She is a native of Turkey, one of the highest Muslim-majority countries in the world. The number of Christians is less than 1 percent of the population, so when she decided to follow Jesus, she knew it wouldn't be easy.

"I don't regret saying yes that day. I only regret the twenty years I lived without Him," she told me.

She led her would-be husband to Christ. It started with a Bible in her hands, and he asked her what it was. Semse said it was a letter from God and "I'm a postman." She gave him the Bible and her phone number.

He later converted and became passionate about sharing his faith. The two married. All the while, his family rejected him and were embarrassed by him. He lost many of his friends. But the young couple didn't care.

"When God calls you, you cannot say no. It's far better to

walk on water with Jesus rather than stay on the ship and sink," she said.

Her husband spent a month in a local jail on trumped-up charges. Following the example of Paul and Silas in ancient Turkey, he preached to his fellow inmates. They offered him release if only he would deny his faith. He refused. He refused the Islamist lawyer the court system offered him. "My lawyer is Jesus." Miraculously, he was later released.

The two started a church in Eastern Turkey and led a growing congregation. They began to work for a publishing house that produced Christian materials in the Turkey language.

It was a field that had been unchurched, as the entire region was nearly untouched by the gospel and was often hostile toward any attempt to talk about Jesus. Still, they persisted.

The couple talked about their faith in such an environment. "How far will we go?" After all, they now had two young children. They agreed, "even to death."

Eventually that pledge came true. Three employees of the publishing company, including Necati, were murdered, shocking the nation and much of the world. The trial took almost a decade, and the three conspirators were eventually given life terms.

Semse created international headlines when she expressed forgiveness for the murderers. "I never had anger or hatred towards the murderers," she said. In the Islamic world, forgiveness without payment is a foreign concept. It's a sign of weakness. The idea of grace has no literal connection.

"I've been praying for the murderers. I want them to come to Christ as Paul repented in the Bible," she said with all certainty. "I want God to shine through this, his light and glory. I want them to be free from sin."

She was finally granted asylum to the United States in 2014, but her life is less than idyllic. She has trouble with finances, employment, and stability. Semse is trying to provide a stable home for her two children, who need to heal.

"My husband had an opportunity to deny Jesus, and he didn't," she said. "He was faithful to the point of giving up his life. So how can I say no? How can I deny Jesus at this point? I want to be faithful to death, too."

The two of them have said "yes," over and again, despite the worst kind of opposition. "But like Jesus walking with Daniel in the flames, He is here with us now," said Semse.

I realize that telling this story isn't the joyful saga that many of us hope to get by *Living a Life of Yes*. But it needs to be said.

Are you willing to give up everything for the sake of something? Are you ready to start saying "yes"?

10

ARE YOU READY TO SAY "YES"?

"There are many talented people who haven't fulfilled their dreams because they over thought it, or they were too cautious, and were unwilling to make the leap of faith." —James Cameron

I'm not going to lie to you. Every leap of faith is going to have to start with a splash. You can't nudge your way in, dipping a toe or peering over the edge. It's all in or not at all.

That's why the first step is always the biggest step.

"Get up!" Jesus told a sick man. "Pick up your mat and walk" (John 5:8).

"Leave," He told a blind man. "Wash in the Pool of Siloam," Jesus commanded the blind man (John 9:7).

"Come out!" He told Lazarus, a dead man up until that point (John 11:43).

"Sign up," He told my friend who was wavering about going back to school.

"Go across the room," He said to another friend who wanted to make an important connection for work.

"Volunteer," He said to my neighbor friend who wanted to help the elderly.

Get up.

Leave.

Come out.

Sign up.

Go across the room.

Volunteer.

Every miraculous event in life always starts with step one—and that usually requires the most significant leap. After that, the pieces will fall into place, and you'll wonder what took you so long.

What Will Be Your First "Yes"?

Since I've been on this journey, I've heard amazing stories of hope. I have been encouraged and emotionally moved. The stories come from all corners of life, and I encounter so many interesting people who are changing the world because they are *Living a Life of Yes.*

There's a time to read and hear about other people, and then there's a time to be like those other people.

I heard a story about a couple who had such a moment in their life when they couldn't use any more excuses, when nearly every piece to the puzzle fell together except for one.

Mike and Lori Salley said "yes," and it forever changed their life.

Mike had a high-paying job with a Fortune 100 company where he climbed the ladder of success, satisfaction, and rewards. He was happy and living the American Dream but felt something was missing.

Now let's just stop the tape because you know where this is headed. He and his wife made a big leap of faith. We'll get to that story in a second.

But let's focus on his lot in life. He had a beautiful house, financial security, and a job that satisfied him. He was being groomed for a vice-president's role with his company. He was involved in local ministry and life . . . was good. There was no incentive to go looking for something else.

There are plenty of people who "just say yes" because their lives aren't offering them a lot of options. I get that. I've done the same thing. I said "yes" because saying "no" meant more of the same boring, humdrum life. There are times when I've said "yes" because there was no other option. God can use that.

But saying "yes" when you have options, that's huge. That might be you.

And that was the story of Mike and Lori's life.

Mike felt the urge to "do something" at a worship service one night in Kansas City, Missouri. When God was nudging Mike, it was almost like He was giving him a choice.

"The interesting thing was that it was presented to me in a way that was optional. It wasn't something I absolutely had to do, but more like an opportunity. It was an open door."

He continued with the nudge, and eventually it became a whisper, and before long it became a scream to "do something."

"I only knew it would involve some sort of physical move in our near future."

He had no idea where he would go, what he would do, or what it would look like. "We didn't have a plan, something that was very difficult for me as someone who likes to know the direction my life is going. Whatever it was, I felt there would be a shift in our lives that would be both exciting and very scary."

But there was a first step that had to be taken.

So, they put their house up for sale.

"I had no idea what we would do if we sold it. Visions of us living in my parents' trailer or deer camp were just a few of the many ideas that were traversing through my mind. What if we sold the house and had no place to go? What would my employees or my boss think if they saw our house was for sale? What in the world would I tell them? I had no answer for that question."

Mike did what I would do—and probably you too. He asked for a sign.

Who can blame Mike? Sure, Jesus dismissed those who always wanted Him to produce a sign. How about another miracle? Another trick? But He wasn't a genie or a magician, and He saw through their impure thoughts and immaturity.

But asking for a sign if you are ready, open, and willing is another thing. With an obedient heart, God loves to give signs. I think He almost delights in them.

"I was praying, and I asked the Lord, 'If I am supposed to sell our home, please give me a sign and I will do it.' At that very moment, a picture popped into my mind. It was a picture of a 'For Sale by Owner' sign. However, there was something very different about this sign. It was like nothing I had ever seen. On this sign, the word 'Owner' was marked out with a Ghost Busters type symbol, and it was replaced by the word 'God.' For Sale by God. Well, I did ask for a sign, and He showed me an actual sign."

Mike could have just swallowed this as some sort of craziness.

But he stood at the edge—and jumped into the complete unknown with absolute abandon.

"I purchased a sign and made the adjustments to it by replacing the word 'owner' with 'God,' and stuck it in our yard waiting for the inevitable fallout."

He had no idea what he would tell his neighbors, friends, or family. He had employees—and a boss. No one had been privy to any of Mike and Lori's leadings.

The house would sell, and it was the first step to a remarkable journey that would eventually land them in Uganda.

Mike and Lori now head a ministry called Show Mercy International, which reaches out to the most vulnerable of people in Uganda.

Somewhere you must find it in yourself to say the first "yes."

I'm Diving In

There's a fantastic YouTube video called "Ten Meter Tower" that is the result of an experiment by Swedish filmmakers Maximilien Van Aertryck and Axel Danielson.[1] It's a mere sixteen minutes, but the riveting footage reflects the back-and-forth, often indecisive nature of humans. It records the intersection of cautious resistance with higher levels of brave impulses.

The subtitle is, "Would you jump? Or would you chicken out?"

The filmmakers found sixty-seven people who were paid to jump off a thirty-three-foot diving board into a pool. The participants had to climb the maze of stairs, march down the diving board, and jump in. That's it.

They filmed the experiment with six cameras and multiple microphones. One by one the participants went to the top, and the doubt in many was quite evident. Some were terrified. Some were simply hesitant.

The audio by the participants is a soundtrack to humanity itself.

"Uh-oh," a young girl says, looking down. And then she walks backward. One young boy goes right to the edge and then backs down. "It's impossible." One teenager admits, "Don't get me wrong, but it's higher than it looks." Another woman throws her hands up and says, "Forget it." Finally, a young girl says, "Alright. Let's do this." And off she goes. Two teens join each other on the board, fist bumping and full of courage. Until they look down. One admits, "It's impossible." The other says, "My heart says 'go,' but my head says 'no.'"

What I loved about this video is how much I saw myself—and others I know—in it.

We are ready to make a difference, but that voice of reason is right there. For me, that voice sounds an awful lot like my mother. Although she was the strongest person I know, she continually urged her children to take it easy. "Count the cost," she would say.

Reasonability is almost an American tradition. It's a survival technique.

Steven Curtis Chapman sings a song called "Dive" that has moved me every time I have wanted to step back from the edge.

At some point, you've got to get to the edge of the diving board and just "jump."

For you, that day might be today.

Ready to Launch

What is the thing you've kept close to your heart? What's the dream that you've tucked away under your pillow? What's the one thing that keeps you going in the darkest of days? Whether it's writing a novel, starting a business, or launching a ministry, somehow you must begin to allow those thoughts to penetrate your mind and start to take root. And then you must be brave enough to talk about it, to unleash it.

So, right now, tell someone your dream. Stop reading, pick up the phone, and share it.

It might start with your best friend, or your spouse, or a trusted confidant. Start talking it up. The more you talk, the better you'll be able to frame the options. Sometimes by talking things through you can sort out the crazy idea from the one that just might work.

I've worked in public relations and communications for many years. We work hard to pack the most amount of content in the fewest amount of words. The more you work on an idea and the more you sort it out, the more clarity you'll get. Eventually you'll be able to tell the whole story in thirty seconds—and make it sound good. Some talk about the "elevator pitch." This is the idea that you have ten floors to pitch your idea to an executive or a decision maker. It's a great tool to help you bring your big idea into a few well-placed sentences.

As I worked through concepts for this book, I didn't just type them out and call them good. I talked about them with friends and family. I shared them with people. Sometimes even strangers got a "test question" from me.

There will be people who will tell you it won't work, those same wonderful souls who think their gift is "practicality." On the other hand, you'll have people who are perpetual cheerleaders, who never met an idea they didn't think was "awesome" and "perfect." You don't need people like that either.

You need confidants, genuine friends, who will not just validate your ideas but help you see hidden roadblocks and then help you clear them with logic, prayer, and action.

How to Say "Yes"

My friend Chris is always game for adventure. There's no challenge he backs down from. There's no game he won't play. There's no mountain he won't climb. But he's always ready to serve.

He lived in the Houston area and was ready for the predicted rain before Hurricane Harvey. He dug ditches around his property and laid rock against the soft spots in his lawn. He had food and water on hand in case he had to dig in. His family was secure. But his care and concern didn't stop there.

He thought about his responsibility to those around him. He outfitted his Land Rover for deep-water driving, just in case he needed to rescue a neighbor. He ran a pipe from his exhaust to above his roofline. He had ropes and hooks and canoes ready to go.

And a lot of other Texans deployed big trucks and boats in equally selfless matters to seek out the needy. Chris's wife Melissa made sure they had food and bedding ready at the house for guests. They were ready to "jump into the water" to help. Because that's what they do.

For some, like Chris, saying "yes" is easy. It's not a far step from the uncertain to the impossible. But for others, the step is a giant leap.

I love this advice from Google executive Eric Schmidt:

Find a way to say yes to things. Say yes to invitations to a new country, say yes to meet new friends, say yes to learn something new. Yes is how you get your first job, and your next job, and your spouse, and even your kids. Even if it's a bit edgy, a bit out of your comfort zone, saying yes means that you will do something new, meet someone new, and make a difference. Yes lets you stand out in a crowd, be the optimist, see the glass full, be the one everyone comes to. Yes is what keeps us all young.

Think of all the places "yes" has already taken you. If you are in a relationship, you at some point said "yes"—and hopefully your spouse or boyfriend or girlfriend said the same thing! And this is something you'll keep saying "yes" to. With every slightly negative interaction or even the biggest fight, at the end of it you will continue to say "yes." When the hair falls out or grows gray or even in new places, both of you keep saying "yes."

If you are employed, both you and your employer said "yes." And that "yes" continues even though the raise is paltry or your performance is not always at its best.

We say "yes" to new purchases, to the clothes we wear, to the food we eat . . . to something, in every moment of every day.

Mouthing those words or embedding the thought isn't really such a tough thing.

Forget the Clock

I know what's going through your mind. Like those people on the end of the diving board. "But. But. But."

I want you to forget the clock. How old you are has no relevance to anything. I've told you stories about the young making significant changes. And I've told you stories about older people making a difference too. The truth is, you don't need to read it in this book. There are people in your world who are saying "yes." Find them out. Let their courage rub off on you. They are the difference makers, and you need to be in their path.

It doesn't matter how long you've been putting off this call to action. In Greek there are two words for time. One is *chronos*, and that's the word we use for our modern timekeeping terms like "chronological." It's the sequential *tick-tick-tick* of a clock and calendar. The other word is *kairos*, and that indicates an opportunity, a proper moment for action.

Kairos is also the kind of time God is most interested in. As He weaves in and out of eternity, His timing is always perfect. It doesn't always make sense, but it's always perfect.

"Now is the time," is a call to kairos. This kind of moment might not make a bit of sense in our linear world, but I'm hoping you will look to another kind of timeline.

Forget the Map

I also hope you will forget the map. We use maps to help us figure out where we are and where we should go. I realize that map skills, traditional latitude and longitude vectoring of our place in this world, has been supplanted by GPS coordinates. But when you call up Google or Apple Maps, they are simply looking at your device, and they use satellites to plot out the coordinates for you.

I guess in a way they can use a map to plot out where you've been, but only you can talk about what those locations really meant to you. I've been lost in the woods—with no map and no GPS. I had to carefully observe my surroundings and accurately retrace my steps to find my way back.

Sometimes we must walk up the mountain, only to discover that the path is blocked. Sometimes we take three steps forward and then two steps back.

The Jews wandered for forty years. At no time were they more than a week's walk away from their destination. They were lost.

I've been lost physically in a car, in a strange city. I've been lost emotionally, wrung with sadness and guilt. I've been lost spiritually, trading in my hope for a few pieces of silver.

I haven't always been lost, but sometimes I've been stagnant, which is simply being a dot on a map.

As you look around, you are surrounded by a world that you probably didn't create. In some ways, you don't know how you got there. Often you don't know how to get out.

But all of that doesn't matter, because you have places to go and things to do.

Forget the Mirror

And finally, as you get ready to plunge, I implore you to ignore the mirror. Whatever that reflection tells you, there's another story.

The New Testament story of Peter reveals a deeply flawed man who disqualified himself at almost every turn. He refused to accept the idea of another kingdom, instead wanting to lead the zealots into an overthrow of the Roman government. That was his idea of kingdom come. He just couldn't get the concept of peaceful, spiritual conquest. And despite his great bravado, he couldn't stay awake in the garden. When he awoke, he was ready to fight.

The night prior he had bragged that he would never leave,

that he alone would stand until the very end. And then the cock crowed for the third time, and Peter had already melted into the crowd.

But then a few days later, Jesus cooked him breakfast on the shore. It was a loving, restorative act of mercy and forgiveness. It was a chance to pick up the pieces and the clay and put together the rock that would later lead the church.

After that transformative moment, he would say "yes" at every opportunity right up until his martyrdom. He forgot the mirror with all its flaws and chose to see himself as Jesus had seen him.

There all kinds of people in the Bible with bad reflections in the mirror. There are poorly qualified people in our world today. Their self-perception is bad. And what others perceive might be even worse.

But that's not who you are. When Samuel went down the line of Jesse in picking a future king, he finally chose the runt of the family. He was puny, even helpless looking. God told Samuel that He looks at the heart, while man looks at the outward appearance. That's still true today.

But we see what others see—Goliath thinking, "They're sending a child?" (1 Samuel 17:42).

Or me, a government worker. Or you—a housewife, a student, a retiree, a divorcée.

Things are rarely as they seem. The mirror lies. We may look disqualified, broken, and unusable. And still, God reaches down and says, "You are chosen."

Ripple Effect

> *"Let there be light" (Genesis 1:3).*

The first recorded expression of all time was just four simple words.

There wasn't anyone around to hear. No creation could witness their expression. We don't know if they were implied or a simple thought. But something tells me they were roared, an audio file that blasted the speakers of the formless and void universe.

There is a beauty and a simplicity in these words, almost poetic as God often seems when He gives the Word. He doesn't need to explain or justify. He doesn't need to split hairs or explain what He really means.

He doesn't need an explanatory phrase like "right now." Nor does He need an adjective like "bright."

That's the stuff we would do. "Let there be bright, amazing light, this very second—and I mean it!"

He just spoke, and it was done. His word was enough.

And as he flipped that switch in a darkened universe, illumination was evoked. And here we are, light years later, and one by one the orbs are igniting, one galaxy after another, like a house with rooms that know no end.

That's what happens when we bring light. We illuminate darkened minds. We help push away misunderstanding and sadness and confusion, and we change the world.

The ripple effects of *Living a Life of Yes* may never be known fully. For generations, even light years away, lights are still being turned on.

One example is the conversion of Billy Graham, the man who led millions to Christ and changed the entire culture. Let's rewind the tape of history back to 1856 to a Sunday school teacher who was talking to a young man named Dwight L. Moody. That teacher, Edward Kimball, said this: "I can truly say . . . that I have seen few persons whose minds were spiritually darker than was his when he came into my Sunday school class."[2]

Still, Kimball persisted. Moody said "yes" and not only accepted the call on his life but became the foremost evangelist of the nineteenth century.

At one of Moody's meetings at Lake Forest College, J. Wilbur Chapman met with the evangelist, who assured him of his faith and helped cement Chapman's resolve. He too became an evangelist.

Chapman would later hire a young Billy Sunday as an assistant to help organize evangelistic meetings. Sunday himself would go on to become a dynamic preacher.

Billy Sunday held an evangelistic campaign in Charlotte, North Carolina, in 1924, and a Christian businessman's club would spring out of that revival.

That club would influence a man named Mordecai Ham.

Ham would later lead his own gospel meetings, and at a 1934 gathering, Billy Graham went forward and the twentieth century was forever changed.

You just never know where things will lead. You never know where an interest will lead. You never know what a passion will inspire. You never know who else you will motivate.

11

THESE PEOPLE ARE LIVING A LIFE OF YES

"If you think adventure is dangerous, try routine. It is lethal."
—Paulo Coelho

I certainly have very few skills beyond my words. But I am trying to find ways to put these to work, to help encourage those who are making a difference on the ground. And there are other abilities I have, but I am not skilled. I can swing a hammer, but don't ask me to erect a wall, unless you want it to wobble. I can spend time, talking and listening. I can just show up. Those aren't specialties—just using what I have.

We can seek those who are hurting, to help give a pick-me-up just when they are ready to fall. We can be part of a bigger story. We can stand and cheer.

Use what you have.

I have met a few other people on this journey who are purely saying "yes" with their abilities. You won't read about these people or see them on the national news. They are people whom I've met during the writing of this book—and every day I'm meeting more.

Meet Michelle Senters, Dan King, Carina McConaughey, Stephanie Riggs, and Christopher Conway.

I can hardly wait to add your story to the list.

Send Joy

I don't know about you, but my elementary school art was less than world changing. I would bring home a drawing, a painting, or a project and proudly present it to my mom. And of course it went on the refrigerator with all the others until the magnet wouldn't hold.

My mother kept everything. My school pictures. My report cards. My birthday cards. Funny, she never kept my artwork.

As I've aged, my art hasn't improved. Even simple drawings bring quizzical looks from others. "Is this some sort of impressionist art?" "Um, no. It's a dog and a car."

I wish I would have had Michelle Senters as a teacher. There are few Picassos in the third grade. But this art instructor has found a creative way to inspire her students to aspire to greatness beyond the refrigerator.

Shielding children from bad news is almost impossible these days. Early 2017 was a nonstop barrage of bad news. Hurricanes hit Puerto Rico, Florida, and Texas. The Las Vegas massacre was particularly brutal and impactful. And then there were fires in California that wiped out 1,500 homes.

"Like many adults, I asked, 'What can I do?'" she told me.

"I'm on a teacher's salary, so I'm not able to make a huge financial contribution. I can't even give blood because I'm anemic. But I can write a letter. I can give a good word."

And Michelle also helped her students reach out to impacted people. She has found a way to take her skills, impart then to children, and then make a difference in the world. Michelle is using what she has right where she is.

Michelle had her students find ways to use their artistic abilities to encourage the encouragers. They adopted workers at a hospital in Florida, letter carriers in Houston, and 911 operators in Las Vegas. The children worked on hundreds of six-inch square pieces of artwork that were sent to these individuals.

"I had them think about what makes them happy, what gives them joy. And then I had them draw or paint what was in their minds, in their hearts," she said.

It doesn't have to be complicated. It can be as simple as a child's drawing that can impact a stranger.

Get Out of the Pew

My friend Dan King was an IT manager for a big telecommunications company. He fixed problems as only those guys can. And he was good.

But his life changed trajectory when he started living a life of "yes." He found himself in Haiti after their devastating earthquake in 2010. He wrote about it, calling himself The Unlikely Missionary. He went from "Pew Warmer" to "Poverty Fighter."

"Through that first trip, and other mission trips, God just really kept building my heart for caring for the orphaned and fatherless," he said.

That heart later led him and his wife to say "yes" to adopting a child. And they kept adopting. They will soon have adopted three children to add to the two children they had biologically.

Maybe adoption isn't for you. That's fine. Nor do you have to go to flood zones. You don't have to save the whole world. But it is imperative to do *something*.

There are problems all around us. Pick one. Don't just send your thoughts and prayers, but do something. As Bob Goff says, "Love does."[1]

Sifting through Ashes

The smell of scorched earth permeated everything. It was dirty; the soot of incinerated dreams was everywhere. And it was sad beyond emotion. But helping her friend dig in this ashen wasteland of a burned home changed Carina McConaughey's life.

She's a friend I've had since high school. Her home was one of those threatened by the Angora Fire, an aggressive mountain blaze near Lake Tahoe that in 2007 took out 242 residences and sixty-seven commercial structures, and damaged thirty-five other homes. Every other home around Carina's was destroyed, reduced to smoldering heaps of gray. She stood with her next-door neighbor, gazing at her still-standing fireplace, an ironic tribute to the blaze that evicted the residents who lived in this beautiful forested neighborhood.

Although Carina's home was spared, she wasn't content to bask in her good fortune. She and her husband, Scott, went to work.

Scott, a cabinet maker, fashioned a couple frames, mitered them, and put a heavy-duty screen in the middle. It was lightweight, yet durable enough for the task.

Carina and friends scooped up the ash from one home after another, looking for any remains from the homes that could be spared. They found various odds and ends, fragments of a lifetime. Amazingly, her neighbor found her grandmother's china, untouched and still in perfect condition. And then a round hard object got caught in Carina's improvised screen. She blew the ash off the item to find a gold band. It was her friend's wedding ring.

Within a few weeks of the firestorm, some perennials began popping their heads up through the soil, pushing away the blackened stems with new life. Carina and other neighbors dug up the shoots and repotted them in hundreds of gallon pots. They later replanted them in front of the rebuilt homes that next year.

"It was our gift to our neighbors, a link to the past. Within those ashes were miracles," said Carina.

It's tempting to quit. You're tapped out on caring. I get it. I've been there. Professional fundraisers call it "compassion fatigue." If they're raising money for flood victims, the last thing they want to compete against is a terrorist attack or another natural disaster, because people stop caring. There is a natural temptation to expend only so much concern and then quit. That's it.

But what if it were you on the end of the line, the last in a long string of disasters, and no one cared?

Remember the California fires of 2017. They were poorly named. Someone dubbed them the Wine Country Fires, making the disaster sound like it only affected the aristocrat, evoking the same kind of emotion that a Wall Street Flood or a Malibu Earthquake or a Manhattan Tornado (yes, this is possible in Manhattan, Kansas) might.

But these fires didn't just impact the rich. Thousands of

middle-class and poor people were affected, as well as scores of immigrant workers. Forty-two people died. More than 8,400 structures burned with $1 billion in damage. It was one of the greatest natural disasters in state history, only to be outdone by the blazes of 2018.

Searchers found victims in the ashes, unidentifiable except through medical tagging. I read of one man who was identified only through the serial number on his hip replacement. These are not wealthy wine barons. These are grandparents, neighbors, friends.

Carina, now a seasoned ash sifter from her own experience in her neighborhood, headed into the California burn zone in 2017, armed with ten screens that she and her husband had constructed. She was merely going to help people in any way possible.

There's something beautiful about helping someone dig through the ashes of their life, to help them find some remnant of who they are. And to stand side by side with a friend—or a stranger—at this moment can be powerful.

Compassion doesn't depend on anyone else. In my home, I hope we will no longer talk about disaster zones, government response, or anything else. We will just *do*.

I'm Just One Person

Stephanie Riggs is an Emmy Award–winning, seasoned journalist based in the Denver area. She's been a news anchor and reporter for more than two decades, working at local television stations around the nation. She is also a contributing correspondent to *CBS Sunday Morning* with Jane Pauley and the Christian

Broadcast Network. Her stories go far beyond informing and entertaining.

Stephanie credits her longevity in a tight, competitive business and just about every award you can win in television news to saying "yes" to God.

"From the very beginning of my career," she told me, "I made a decision to pray to God every morning for direction. As a result, the Holy Spirit led me down the road less traveled."

By deciding to say "yes" to Jesus, her entire focus changed and so did the world. She went to places no one wanted to go and in doing so offered a voice to those who might not have had one.

She has revealed hidden stories, inspired people, and helped change the world one story, one person, at a time.

One of her reports featured a West African village that was being supported by one of its own villagers who had ventured to America to find work and sent nearly every penny back home. After his brutal murder by white supremacists in 1997, Stephanie reported on the man's efforts. Her reporting sparked a movement resulting in hundreds of thousands of dollars contributed to improving his village—including a fresh water system, health care, education, and much more. A nonprofit organized nearly twenty years ago, as a result of her report, is still active today.

One of her *CBS Sunday Morning* reports focused on a Colorado couple who made a commitment to care for orphans in one of the most remote parts of eastern Africa more than fifty years ago. It's estimated that more than one million orphans are alive today because of their efforts. Stephanie's single report inspired people to send money to this couple, resulting in tripling the number of orphans being saved.

Recently, Riggs resurrected the hidden history surrounding WASPs—Women Airforce Service Pilots. The contribution of this band of brave women who helped win World War II is left out of our history books. Stephanie's story brought to light their achievements, including finally receiving a Congressional Gold Medal.

Stephanie also said "yes" to taking a compassionate look at the nationwide epidemic of childhood obesity. In her own one-hour television documentary, a group of children and their families get healthy, and those children, now adults, are college athletes and teaching another generation to be fit, thanks to *Fitting In*, which aired on ABC Family.

After reporting on the death of a little person in downtown Denver, Riggs began to delve into the life of dwarfism. She wrote a book and produced a documentary seen around the world called *Never Sell Yourself Short*.

Stephanie also followed the remarkable journey of Lexi and Sydney Stark, who were born on March 9, 2001, conjoined at the base of their spines. Stephanie shared on the CBS program *48 Hours* how these sisters overcame incredible odds. From conception to birth to a risky separation surgery at seven months old to finally two independent, healthy little girls. Today they are getting ready to go to college and are a constant reminder of the power of prayer and how their parents saying "yes" to God changed their lives.

Stephanie is a woman who embodies the word "yes."

"I never thought of myself as a world changer, but God did," she told me. "I just said yes and was always open to adventures and challenges. I knew I wanted to be a reporter from as far back as I can remember, and there were many tests over twenty-plus years, but I refused to quit, and I am so glad

I did. God just made it all happen beyond my wildest dreams!"

According to Stephanie, the pressure is off when you say "yes."

"Seek Him first and His righteousness, because He promises everything will be added to you," she said, quoting Matthew 6:33. "It's all a divine setup! God designed us, He knows the plans He has for us, not to harm us but to prosper us and to give us a hope and a future. So why bother asking anyone else? Pray and get ready for the adventure of a lifetime."

I asked Stephanie if she needed the affirmation of others to say "yes." Shaking her head, she said, "No way."

"My question is, what are you waiting for?" she said. "Don't listen to people. Listen to the still, small voice. God wants to take you to places you have never dreamed. He just needs a yes!"

Every story leads to another story which leads to another story. Even though she was just one person, she kept saying "yes."

Building Up Lives by Breaking Down Mattresses

Christopher Conway is the president and founder of Spring Back Colorado, a social enterprise mattress recycling facility.

Since 2012, Spring Back has recycled more than 381,000 mattresses and box springs.

That's just a dent in the twenty million mattresses and foundations hauled to landfills every year. End to end, that yearly number would circle the globe.

"For most people, it's out of sight, out of mind. They just take it to the dump," said Conway.

And mattresses don't do well in landfills. They are made

from material that takes a long time to break down, and because of their bulk and built-in memory, they continually rise to the top of the pile.

"Landfills have got to the point where they don't see the intrinsic value of taking mattresses, so they are raising prices trying to limit and eliminate that product from their waste stream," said Conway.

As an alternative, Spring Back disassembles the mattresses and resells the components—steel, foam, fiber, and wood—and resells the material.

In the last seven years, Spring Back has recycled three million pounds of steel and another 3.5 million pounds in cotton and foam materials. Any residual wood by-product is mulched.

The recycled commodities market is currently depressed, so the operation can't run solely on funds received from the resale of the products. The shifting sands of the secondary market challenges "the trash train."

Add to that the cost to run heavy machinery, trucking goods, facility outlays, and labor, and the operation is expensive to run. They do receive grants, but that doesn't stop Conway from looking for efficiencies and productivity and the best bang for the buck in the marketplace.

"Any grants or gifts we get don't change my life, and they don't change the employees' lives, but they do allow us to expand and look for new opportunities."

While their recycling mission resonates with a culture that is increasingly cognizant of the environmental impact of waste, Conway's primary purpose is helping repurpose lives.

"At the core of what we do is to take men in recovery and give them redemptive employment opportunities," said Conway.

In our society, one of the most significant issues is recidivism—a reentry into the prison system. But if you've ever worked with someone who is trying to reset their life after they've been arrested, incarcerated, and released, you know it's not easy.

The ongoing personal and financial cost of reentry into society is exasperating. In many cases, you cannot drive, and yet you are expected to work. Those in recovery will receive unannounced drug tests that interrupt a regular work schedule, and without a vehicle, it's a major inconvenience to an employer.

And the simple path is to go back to prison. That is what first got Conway to consider moving beyond charity and instead building character by providing opportunity.

"I saw so many of these men who were hopeless. They had stopped using drugs and alcohol and went out into the community to find employment but were disqualified because our society is not felon friendly," said Conway. "So I decided to put my marker down and offer a chance for felons to have gainful employment."

Spring Back helps the practical barriers that most convicts face, such as court fees and costs for drug tests. But those are temporary measures, something that is simply enabling. So Conway takes it up a notch.

"Most of all, we give these men gainful employment so that they can take care of some of their responsibilities in life, giving them a new beginning."

Conway is up-front about his own convictions and intentions. "We give them a support system of faith, family, and friends. We're not trying to sell anything. We want them to enhance their belief systems."

"Recovery is hard enough on its own, but without a center,

something that it all revolves around, it's nearly impossible. For me, it's a Christ center."

He says the men who work at Spring Back are "among the finest people I've ever been in contact with." Yet nearly every one of them is an addict—heroin, methamphetamine, or alcohol dependent.

"They just can't get through life without some sort of additive," said Conway. "But no one wants to be a drug addict. The only difference between these men and most of us are just a couple of bad decisions."

Throughout the years, more than 163 men have worked at Spring Back. There have been successes and failures. But Conway keeps the expectation modest.

"Quite simply, we try to fill our men with hope. We want to give them a chance to reformat their families, their bodies, and their responsibilities."

As an example, he offers the success of a long-term employee named Timothy who recently got his own apartment and now provides housing for his wife and child. He also was able to get his own driver's license.

One of the goals for employees is posted in the workroom. "Get a job, get a better job, get a career." It's all about what the men choose to make of their lives, and Spring Back gives that opportunity.

For Conway, the entire Spring Back operation has been about saying "yes"—even when it was uncomfortable.

"I remember saying 'yes' to the pastor of my church who asked us to move an inch out of our comfort zones," he said.

That led to volunteering at local homeless shelters.

That opened him up to contacting a similar recycling

program in Nashville after it was featured on National Public Radio.

"I said 'yes' to visiting them. And then I said 'yes' to develop a mattress recycling facility."

"I continually said 'yes' and seldom said 'no.'"

Conway is encouraging others to get off the well-worn paths of comfort. At age fifty, he had to learn a whole new business model. He had to learn about court systems and addictions and how to help an entire class of people navigate a system that was unfamiliar to him.

"We're very comfortable traveling in that well-worn path, seldom deviating. I encourage you to say 'yes.' Take a chance! Don't stay status quo. Take a chance on doing something unknown. Be open to being a beginner."

He believes in staying open to uncertainty.

"I had to say 'yes' to opportunities that I never dreamed of. I had to say 'yes,' that I would help others in need. I had to say 'yes' to learn about homelessness, drug addiction, and alcoholism."

None of that was necessarily comfortable, but it was necessary.

"'No' is the easy way out. But 'yes' is the critical word to what's happened here. 'Yes' has been very transformative to me," he said.

The change has been how he sees himself and others.

"It's my job to serve and respond to the needs and not sit in judgment about how someone got into their situation," said Conway. "So, hand the man with a sign three or five dollars and by doing so we start a chain of fifteen cars at a stoplight all giving to one human being. This would be a movement of 'yes.'"

"'Yes' is the critical word, these three letters can change our lives and that of others."

That's what I'm finding in this great adventure too.

I can create plans and scenarios, but ultimately it comes down to simply stepping up and doing what's right. The rest will come.

12

THE BOOK ENDS, BUT YOUR LIVING BEGINS

"In the end, it's not the years in your life that count. It's the life in your years." —Abraham Lincoln

If I could go back in time, there's plenty I would change. If the thirty-year-old me could speak a little sanity into the fifteen-year-old me, I could have avoided plenty of teenage drama.

If the forty-year-old me could have interjected some wisdom into the thirty-year-old me, I would have altered my focus.

Who knows what the eighty-year-old me would say to me today?

I think at every juncture I would have encouraged myself to exercise more, eat less, spend more time with my children, and nurture my marriage relationship more. I would have suggested more friends in my life, deeper church connections, and stronger connections to people outside my usual circle.

But most of all, I wish I would have learned this principle of "yes" earlier in my life.

I think about all the life I missed, the relationships I bypassed, the adventures that passed me by.

I wish I would have learned the joy of planting a seed of "yes."

The Seed of "Yes"

One of the miracles of nature is that of the seed.

I'm trying to be a home gardener. I'm always fighting the cold and the heat, the bugs and the blight. Still I persist. And I don't like buying starter plants from the nursery. I want to buy the seeds, put them in small pots, water them, and let them sit in the window.

This method isn't without frustration. One spring, after four weeks of watching indoor sprouts take off, I moved my trays outside in the sun. At some point, a gust of wind flipped my babies in the air, and they spilled to the ground. The garden was over before it even started.

But when it works, the synergy of soil, water, and sun never ceases to impress me. I love to take my plants from seed to harvest and from harvest to table. Eating a tomato that months earlier was a flat, oval-shaped seed is stunning to me. And the fact that my little seed produced a massive plant with dozens of fruits hanging from the vine takes my breath away at the elegant complexity of it all.

Some seeds spread naturally, without any intervention by humans. Those are truly the miracle seeds.

Like parachutists from an airplane, traveling the earth's currents and breezes, some seeds float on high, looking to colonize a distant mountain or fertile valley.

That's what people who are *Living a Life of Yes* can do. Their seeds of optimism, faith, and hope don't just grow plants in their own backyard. They can spread to a neighborhood, a family, a city, a church, and even the world.

I'm asking you to say "yes."

Just drop one seed into a cup. Put it in a little soil, and let the sun and water soak in.

You'll find the harvest is always greater than the seed.

The challenge awaits you.

The 14-Day Living a Life of Yes Challenge

I'm going to ask you to do something far more life-changing than dumping a bucket of ice water on your head. I'm asking you to go above and beyond a discipline like swearing off chocolate for lent or carbs for the summer.

I want you to say "yes" for 14 days. That's it. Every uncomfortable situation, you dive in. Every new door, you open it. Every opportunity, you lay aside your excuses and say "yes."

You might want to do this with others. Find a friend or two, and challenge each other. Compare your fears and frustrations. Celebrate your successes.

Maybe you won't change the world, but you'll start to change your life.

What's your next courageous step? It might seem small, but it will be huge in your heart.

If you start *Living a Life of Yes*, you'll meet new people and realize what an amazing, diverse world this is. You'll expand your mind, exercising the risk muscle that only gets stronger and wiser. You'll defy the years, as the experiences will keep you young. You'll be fresh, full of new perspective and insight.

If you start *Living a Life of Yes*, you'll never be the same.

But it must start somewhere. It must start sometime.

So why not today?

Go to www.LiveAYesLife.com and share your video story or write your adventure. You can also communicate through at Stories@LiveAYesLife.com.

Now it's your turn.
We want to hear about how you are Living a Life of Yes.
The little stories.
The big stories.
They all matter.
They all make a difference.
Share your story at LiveAYesLife.com.

Connect with us on Facebook at Living a Life of Yes.
For comments or questions contact Info@DavidRupert.com.
To book David for an interview or speaking event,
contact events@DavidRupert.com.

NOTES

2. Find a Way to Dream Again

1. .Craig Impelman, "Make Each Day Your Masterpiece," www.TheWoodenEffect.com, published January 18, 2017, https://www.thewoodeneffect.com/your-masterpiece/.
2. .Matthew West, "Do Something," lyric video, Sparrow Records, 2014, https://www.youtube.com/watch?v=b_RjndG0IX8.
3. .J. B. Phillips, *Your God Is Too Small* (New York: Macmillan Paperbacks, 1961).
4. .Myrna Oliver, "Larry Walters: Soared to Fame on Lawn Chair," *Los Angeles Times*, November 24, 1993, http://articles.latimes.com/1993-11-24/news/mn-60236_1_larry-walters.
5. ."History and Rules," www.DarwinAwards.com, https://darwinawards.com/rules/rules1.html.

3. Beyond Thoughts and Prayers

1. .Deidra Riggs, *One: United in a Divided World* (Grand Rapids, MI: Baker Books, 2017).

4. What's Your Excuse?

1. .Rich Shapiro and Corky Siemaszko, "Relatives of Charleston Shooting Victims Offer Forgiveness to Dylann Roof in First Court Appearance: 'Their Legacies Will Live in Love, So Hate Won't Win,'" *New York Daily News*, June 20, 2015, https://www.nydailynews.com/news/national/relatives-charleston-shooting-victims-offer-forgiveness-article-1.2264253.
2. .Mark Batterson, *Chase the Lion: If Your Dream Doesn't Scare You, It's Too Small* (New York: Multnomah, 2016).
3. .Jack Shea, "Girls' Lemonade Stand for Hurricane Harvey Victims Touches Hearts Across Northeast Ohio," Fox8.com, September 6, 2017, https://fox8.com/2017/09/06/girls-lemonade-stand-for-hurricane-harvey-victims-touches-hearts-across-northeast-ohio/.

NOTES

4. .Patricia Raybon, "It's Never Too Late," www.PatriciaRaybon.com, October 29, 2016, https://www.patriciaraybon.com/its-never-too-late/.
5. .Russ Wiles, "A Curious Retiree Is a Happy Retiree," *USA Today*, www.USAToday.com, published June 3, 2016, https://www.usatoday.com/story/money/personalfinance/2016/06/03/curious-retiree-happy-retirement-long-term-care-insurance/84815098/.
6. .Henry James, *The Madonna of the Future* (London: Macmillan, 1887), e-book ed., http://www.gutenberg.org/files/2460/2460-h/2460-h.htm.
7. .Brené Brown, *Daring Greatly: How the Courage to be Vulnerable Transforms the Way We give, Love, Parent, and Lead* (New York: Penguin, 2012), 2.

5. Moving Beyond Yesterday

1. .Curt Thompson book quoted in "How Neuroscience—and the Bible—Explain Shame," interview with Curt Thompson by Rob Moll, www.ChristianityToday.com, June 23, 2016, https://www.christianitytoday.com/ct/2016/julaug/how-neuroscience-and-bible-explain-shame.html. Also see Curt Thompson, *The Soul of Shame: Retelling the Stories We Tell About Ourselves* (Downers Grove, IL: InterVarsity, 2015).

6. Overcome the Fear

1. ."America's Top Fears 2018," Chapman University Survey of American Fears, October 16, 2018, https://blogs.chapman.edu/wilkinson/2018/10/16/americas-top-fears-2018/.
2. 1.Brené Brown, *Daring Greatly: How the Courage to be Vulnerable Transforms the Way We give, Love, Parent, and Lead* (New York: Penguin, 2012), 171.
   ."America's Top Fears 2018," Chapman University Survey of American Fears, October 16, 2018, https://blogs.chapman.edu/wilkinson/2018/10/16/americas-top-fears-2018/.
3. .Mark Batterson, *Chase the Lion: If Your Dream Doesn't Scare You, It's Too Small* (New York: Multnomah, 2016), 91.
4. .Mark Batterson, *Chase the Lion*, 92.
5. .Mark Batterson, *Chase the Lion*, 93.
6. .Jeremiah Burroughs, "The Rare Jewel of Christian Contentment: A Quality Abridgement" (Pensacola, FL: Chapel Library, 2010), 63, https://chapellibrary.org:8443/pdf/books/rjoc.pdf.

NOTES

7. Don't Play It Safe

1. .Michael Yaconelli, *Dangerous Wonder: The Adventure of Childlike Faith* (Colorado Springs: NavPress,1998), 72.

8. Get Ready to Change the World

1. .Story about Wright brothers found in Mark Batterson's *In a Pit with a Lion on a Snowy Day: How to Survive and Thrive When Opportunity Roars* (New York: Multnomah, 2016), 195. Also see Wright brothers' letter to the Smithsonian at https://siarchives.si.edu/history/featured-topics/stories/letter-dated-may-30-1899.
2. .Deidra Riggs, "How to Make It Happen," www.DeidraRiggs.com, August 29, 2016, http://www.deidrariggs.com/2016/08/29/how-to-make-it-happen/.

10. Are You Ready to Say "Yes"?

1. .Maximilien Van Aertryck and Axel Danielson, "Ten Meter Tower," produced by Plattform Produktion, published June 29, 2017, https://www.youtube.com/watch?v=cU2AvkKA4kM&t=70s.
2. .Donald G. Mathews, "Dwight L. Moody: American Evangelist, 1837–1899 (review)," *Civil War History* 16, no. 4 (1970): 353–354, https://muse.jhu.edu/article/418936/summary (retrieved January 14, 2019).

11. These People Are Living a Life of Yes

1. .Bob Goff, *Love Does: Discover a Secretly Incredible Life in an Ordinary World* (Nashville: Thomas Nelson, 2012).

ABOUT THE AUTHOR

David Rupert is a Colorado-based writer, speaker, and communicator.

As a communications professional, David has been interviewed more than 1,000 times by various local and regional media as well as national outlets including *Fox News*, *Good Morning America*, and *CNN*. He served for nine years as the chaplain for the nation's 30,000 Postmasters, advising senior leadership, and writing a monthly column for their national publication.

He also served as the editor of one of the nation's largest employee newsletters for eight years, winning many awards.

He was instrumental in forming Writers on the Rock, which has grown to a community of more than 800 writers. The group also hosts an annual gathering which is now the largest one-day Christian writers conference in the nation.

David is currently a featured writer at *Patheos Evangelical*. His works have appeared in more than 20 periodicals. Dozens of national and regional radio outlets have interviewed him on culture, faith, refugees, and politics.

He is an engaging speaker and teacher of a variety of subjects at topics across the nation. Today he's helping men, women, and youth learn the most liberating word in the English language -- "Yes!"

www.ingramcontent.com/pod-product-compliance
Lightning Source LLC
Chambersburg PA
CBHW030112100526
44591CB00009B/374